To Karen,

with best wishes

[signature]

Spiritual Growth

Healing + Wholeness

Transformation

NUMBER SEVEN:
*Carolyn and Ernest Fay Series
in Analytical Psychology*
David H. Rosen, General Editor

*A complete listing of books
in print in this series appears on the last page.*

Transformation

EMERGENCE OF THE SELF

Murray Stein

Foreword by David H. Rosen

TEXAS A&M UNIVERSITY PRESS

COLLEGE STATION

Permission to quote from the following sources was granted by Princeton University Press:
C. G. Jung. *Collected Works.* Copyright © 1953, 1954, 1956 & 1966
by The Bollingen Foundation.
C. G. Jung. *Notes to the Seminar Held 1925* (Analytical Psychology).
Copyright © 1989 by Princeton University Press.
William McGuire, ed., Ralph Manheim & R. F. C. Hull, trans.
The Freud-Jung Letters. Copyright © 1974 by Sigmund Freud Copyrights and
Erbengemeinschaft Prof. Dr. C. G. Jung.
Permission to use illustrations from the *Rosarium,* MS 394a, was granted
by Vadianische Sammlung, Kantonsbibliothek (Vadiana), St. Gallen.

Library of Congress Cataloging-in-Publication Data

Stein, Murray, 1943–
    Transformation : emergence of the self / Murray Stein. — 1st ed.
      p.   cm. — (Carolyn and Ernest Fay series in analytical psychology ; no. 7)
    Includes bibliographical references and index.
    ISBN 0-89096-780-6 (hardcover : alk. paper)
    1. Adulthood—Psychological aspects.   2. Change (Psychology)   3. Self-
actualization (Psychology)   4. Identity (Psychology)   5. Jungian psychology.
6. Psychoanalysis.   7. Jung, C. G. (Carl Gustav), 1875–1961.   I. Title.   II. Series.
BF724.5.S75   1998
155.6—dc21   97-41052
                                                                     CIP

NUMBER SEVEN
Carolyn and Ernest Fay Series
in Analytical Psychology
David H. Rosen, General Editor

The Carolyn and Ernest Fay edited book series, based initially on the annual Fay Lecture Series in Analytical Psychology, was established to further the ideas of C. G. Jung among students, faculty, therapists, and other citizens and to enhance scholarly activities related to analytical psychology. The Book Series and Lecture Series address topics of importance to the individual and to society. Both series were generously endowed by Carolyn Grant Fay, the founding president of the C. G. Jung Educational Center in Houston, Texas. The series are in part a memorial to her late husband, Ernest Bel Fay. Carolyn Fay has planted a Jungian tree carrying both her name and that of her late husband, which will bear fruitful ideas and stimulate creative works from this time forward. Texas A&M University and all those who come in contact with the growing Fay Jungian tree are extremely grateful to Carolyn Grant Fay for what she has done. The holder of the Frank N. McMillan, Jr. Professorship in Analytical Psychology at Texas A&M functions as the general editor of the Fay Book Series.

Wandelt sich rasch auch die Welt
wie Wolkengestalten,
alles Vollendete fällt
heim zum Uralten.

Even if the world changes as fast
as the shapes of clouds,
all perfected things at last
fall back to the very old.

Rilke, *The Sonnets to Orpheus* 1, 19

CONTENTS

ILLUSTRATIONS

FOREWORD

*Transformation: Hymns in innerness, dance before
the ark, uproar and parade in the ripening vine.*
                                        —*Rainer Maria Rilke*

Murray Stein has written a book that, like Jung's work, can help us
to transfigure ourselves, our society, and our global village. Transformation—a subject near and dear to my heart and soul—is the way
to individuation and self-actualization.[1] Rilke put it quite simply:
"You must change your life." Jung emphasized its divine nature:
"There are spiritual processes of transformation in the psyche."[2]

As Jung did, Stein utilizes the butterfly (provided him by a woman
in a "big" dream) to symbolize transformation. In this woman's
dream, which opens chapter 1, the metamorphosis of the caterpillar
is aided by two snakes which are placed into a dark cocoon by a wise
old man. The dreamer knows that she is the caterpillar, and after she
emerges as a butterfly, she miraculously becomes a woman, reborn
as her "true self."

William James stresses that a sudden transformation, so accu-
rately portrayed by the conversion of caterpillar to butterfly, is not
the "miracle" it seems to be, but rather "a natural process."[3] James
also writes about "sick souls" who must be "twice-born" in order
to be happy.[4] The "false self" must die and be shed or molted so
the spiritual change to one's "true self" secondary to the Self (or Supreme Being) can be actualized. Stein describes a person's authentic
self-image, or "imago," as the individual's unique mythic form that
must be fulfilled and realized. His credible contention is that this

most meaningful transformation is the task of the second half of life. Stein's book is all about this natural transformation process. The woman's butterfly dream embodies alchemy, which represents the art of transformation. Symbolically, transmutating lead into gold represents the death-rebirth process leading to one's philosopher's stone and authentic living, as Jung experienced at Bollingen where he was "reborn in stone."

In chapter 1, Stein outlines how transformation develops and proceeds. He uses Rainer Maria Rilke as an example of transformation and healing the soul through creativity. It is the true story of the evolution of Rilke's greatest work, the *Duino Elegies*. Stein also writes eloquently about Jung's transfiguration after his break from Freud.

In chapter 2, he presents an example of transformation, focusing on the metamorphosis of William Mellon, Jr. In mid-life, Mellon went through a transformative experience of giving up his negative dominant ego-image and identity, "false self," and "sick soul" to become a physician and healer of the poverty-stricken sick in Haiti. He named his clinic after Albert Schweitzer, the transformative figure who catalyzed Mellon's transmutation and realization of his philosopher's stone.

In chapter 3, Stein concerns himself with the role of relationships in healing and transformation. He stresses the power of the healing doctor-patient relationship. Stein meaningfully reviews the psychology of the transference à la Jung, which is well illustrated with alchemical pictures from the *Rosarium Philosophorum*. Throughout the chapter Stein comments significantly on marriage and its inner and outer manifestations.

Chapter 4 offers three portraits of transformation: Rembrandt, Picasso, and Jung. This chapter has telling images to accompany the text. Stein makes it very clear that these extremely creative individuals were involved in healing their souls and reflecting back to us needed visions of the essential nature of transformation. Rembrandt's odyssey is a touching view of an evolving divine-self. Stein's treatment of Picasso seems more accurate than Jung's rather negative essay on Picasso.[5] In fact, Stein presents Picasso as an icon of our century, who mirrors back to us a hundred years of world wars and reflects our angst and quest for meaning as this millennium closes. Stein ends chapter 4 of this important book with Bollingen: Jung's awesome self-portrait in stone.

Can we individually and collectively transform so the next millennium will be peaceful, allowing each of us to actualize our potentials as part of one human family in a stable and interdependent global village? In his epilogue, Stein stresses that "it takes a whole village to raise a child." He cites Hillary Rodham Clinton's book on this subject and says hers "is a voice crying in the wilderness." Then he challenges us to get involved in our own transformative experiences. It is true that all transformation begins with each and every one of us. Recall the old adage: Charity begins at home. As Martin Buber stated: "There is meaning in what for long was meaningless. Everything depends on the inner change; when this has taken place, then and only then, does the world change."[6]

David H. Rosen
College Station, Texas

ACKNOWLEDGMENTS

The seeds for this book were sown during a casual conversation I had while taking a walk with Verena Kast. They must have fallen on fertile soil, because they continued to grow in my mind until I was offered the opportunity to present the Carolyn and Ernest Fay Lectures for 1997. By that time, I knew that transformation would be my theme. In a sense, this book is an extension of my earlier work, *In MidLife*, published some fifteen years ago. Also, it offers a theoretical base for my more recent book, *Practicing Wholeness*. While teaching at the Jung Institute of Chicago and lecturing in Mexico City, in Zurich, and at the "Journey into Wholeness" gatherings in North Carolina, I enjoyed rich opportunities for discussing many of the ideas found in the following pages.

I owe debts to so many people who helped me to formulate the ideas and images contained in this book that I am afraid of not naming some of them. Sometimes their contributions were made consciously, sometimes accidentally and indirectly. For help with Rilke, I am grateful particularly to Ruth Ilg on the German text, to Dale Kushner for giving me a glimpse into the inner life of a poet, to David Oswald for useful comments and queries, and to Josip Pasic for a perspective on "pure observation." I have studied Jung for many years and feel grateful to a host of friends, colleagues, and teachers for helping me to gain some degree of understanding of his massive opus; among them are John Beebe, Hilde Binswanger, Michael Fordham, Marie Louise von Franz, Adolph Guggenbühl-Craig, Barbara Hannah, Joseph Henderson, James Hillman, Mario Jacoby, Tom Kirsch, Richard Pope, Lee Roloff, Andrew Samuels, Nathan Schwartz-Salant, June Singer, and Arwind Vasavada. For the inspiration to study the lives and self-portraits of painters for psychological insight, I owe special thanks to Rafael López-Pedraza, Christian Gaillard, and James Wyly. To Jan Marlan, who carefully read an early draft, I owe thanks for her constant encouragement and friendly criticism. For many hours of lively and pleasurable conversation on the subject of transformation, I want to thank my friend Flo Wiedemann. For accurate typing, Bailey Milton is to be praised. Naturally, the Muse must receive a high degree of honor, too.

The book itself I wish to dedicate to Jan, my wife, with whom I have experienced and witnessed the transformation process actively at work for a quarter-century; to my son Christopher, who is in the midst of molting; and to my daughter Sarah, just now a thriving caterpillar.

I am deeply grateful to David Rosen and Carolyn Fay for inviting me to present these lectures. Carolyn Fay has been a source of warmth and support since the early days of my teaching and analytic practice. Her constant dedication to analytical psychology over these decades has been an inspiration to many people, and her life and work bear remarkable witness to the difference that Jung's contribution has made in lives so far removed from the lakes and mountains of Switzerland. David Rosen was the perfect host in College Station, escorting me around the lovely grounds of Texas A&M University, introducing me to his students and colleagues, and making himself available without stint or complaint. His editorial suggestions were a great help in improving the written text. The audience at A&M could not have been more receptive or gracious.

INTRODUCTION

On April 14, 1912, the luxury liner *Titanic* sank on her maiden voyage across the North Atlantic, signaling the end of an era and the beginning of the Age of Anxiety. Also in 1912, as the world unknowingly moved toward the abyss of the first worldwide war in history, the term *transformation* forcefully entered European consciousness, an oracular cry of things to come. It was sounded in the German words *Wandlung* and *Verwandlung*.

In the year 1912, Carl Gustav Jung finished his book, *Wandlungen und Symbole der Libido* (literally, *Transformations and Symbols of Libido*, but translated into English in 1916 as *Psychology of the Unconscious*). This work described the transformational nature of the human psyche and announced Jung's differences with Freud, thus setting him on his own course of personal transformation, through which analytical psychology would be founded. Transformation was a concept that set him irrevocably at odds with his erstwhile teacher and guide.

In the same year, Rainer Maria Rilke heard a line of poetry in the wind that touched off his most important poetical work, the *Duino Elegies*, a ten-part poem that revolves around transformation as the essential human task, as humankind's most important, sacred duty. It is a poem about endings and new beginnings.

And Franz Kafka, in a brief few weeks at the close of 1912, composed his famous story of transformation, "Die Verwandlung" ("Metamorphosis"), a story of degradation in which a human being is changed into a giant insect.

These three figures all were speakers and writers of German, although none of them was a German citizen; one was a genius psychologist and two were brilliant artists (both of whom died at a relatively early age). One was a Protestant, one a Catholic, one a Jew; all three were psychically gifted and psychologically sensitive to the point of fragility. All struck a common chord that would resound through the coming decades: the theme of transformation. Kafka and Rilke would die before the Second World War broke out; Jung would live past it long enough to reflect upon its devastation and to create, in that late period of his life, a great visionary work of wholeness, *Mysterium Coniunctionis*. Today we can see that all three were unintentional prophets and that collectively they provided another name for our now passing century: the Age of Transformation.

The twentieth century has been gripped by global transformation. Massive social, cultural, and political upheavals have erased many of the most prized and familiar features of traditional cultures throughout the world—in Western Europe, the Americas, Russia, Asia, Africa—as two world wars, exploding technologies, and competing ideologies have swept over humanity in wave upon wave of destabilizing energy. This process of global transformation has been represented in the arts, exploited by business, and studied by the social sciences. Its effect upon individuals and upon groups large and small continues to deepen and to expand into every dimension of human life and endeavor. *Liminality* is the constant theme of our times. Nothing is stable and secure. Indeed, as Yeats foresaw, the center has not held.

As we approach the end of this unsettled century, the momentum of change appears to be increasing, and people are preparing for a grand finale that is the end not only of a century but of a millennium. Moreover, this will mark the end of a Platonic Year consisting of twenty centuries—the Age of Pisces—and the beginning of another, the Age of Aquarius. History and myth converge at moments like this, and fears and expectations reach a crescendo. As the rapidity of change accelerates, it becomes evident that no one, not even the people best equipped with the fastest computer networks, can register its myriad details, let alone control them. The times rush ahead like a swollen river, our destination directed by forces beyond our understanding, never mind our control. An end and a beginning are about to coincide.

This is the social and cultural backdrop against which I am presenting this work on psychological transformation. Although I will be focusing primarily on the individual person and on how transformative processes move the individual toward a specific and remarkably precise goal of self-realization, I recognize that there is a profound dynamic interplay between social and political collectives and the individual psyche. Individuals are transforming in large numbers just as (perhaps partly because) large collectives are transforming. It is certainly incorrect to say, as some sociologists and political thinkers have, that individuals merely mirror collective movements and opinions and are nothing but miniature embodiments of social process and structure. On the other hand, it is also misguided to think that individuals are isolated from the larger social settings in which they live, or that psychologically they are structured only by personal experiences in family and kinship groups and by intrapsychic and genetic factors. At this point in our understanding of the formation of psychic structure, it seems most correct to hold that individuals and their destinies are the complex outcome of many combined forces, some of them genetic, others intrapsychic and interpersonal, and still others collective.

By collective, I have in mind not only the specific social, political, and cultural influences that press in upon people, but also the world historical and archetypal shapers and movers that create the zeitgeist of a whole era. The spirit that shapes a historical era also plays a role in shaping the attitudes and visions of individuals. One can argue interminably about zeitgeist and how to represent it for a specific age. It is particularly difficult to identify and describe when one is speaking of one's own time. It is easier to study fourteenth-century Italy and speak of "the Renaissance" or eighteenth-century France and name it "the Enlightenment." When it comes to the twentieth century, however, things become thickly muddled, not only because this period is so close to us but also because the whole world is implicated in the spirit of this particular age. It is hard to grasp something so large and complex.

For the first time in history, wars have been carried out on a global level. The spirit of Ares has swept over all the inhabited continents and drawn them into heated martial engagement with one another. Out of these conflicts have come deep exchanges on all levels, however. When wars end, enemies may become allies or at least trading partners. In my own lifetime, I have watched astonished as this happened first with Germany and Japan, then with Vietnam, and most recently with the states of the former Soviet Union. War brides mix genetic lines in their wombs, and cultures that were opposed on the battlefield end up engaging in commerce and exchanging ideas about religion and the arts. Such processes have had profound effects upon many individuals in modern cultures around the world.

The Greek myth makers had a brilliant insight when they saw Ares, the god of warfare, and Aphrodite, the great love goddess, as mates who create the child Harmonia. What we have witnessed in this dark century of worldwide warfare, ironically, is the birth of a world community. This idea is symbolized in the still highly controversial political idea of a United Nations. It is becoming effectively concretized in multinational corporations. Still in its earliest stages, the notion of a single worldwide human community is showing strong signs of growth and inevitability, even as resistance to it also gathers strength and creates disruptions and turmoil. The twentieth century will go down in history, surely, as the era when integrated one-world consciousness on a global collective level was born. This is not utopian; it is merely stating a fact.

At the same time, we have grown wary of large organizations, collectives, and bureaucracies that attempt to harness the masses and end up stifling the human spirit. As we increasingly recognize the interconnectedness of nations and peoples, we also know that individual initiative, freedom, and responsibility are the key elements of progress and of cultural and social evolution. The world is one, but small is better. We live in a paradox.

This birth of late-twentieth-century consciousness has not been easy. Indeed, it has been a prolonged agony, costing the better part of one hundred years of labor. This is the agony of transformation, typical of a historical period in which familiar, age-old structures break down and a prolonged spell of chaos, confusion, and anxiety ensues. W. H. Auden called ours the Age of Anxiety, and psychoanalysts have served as its priests and rabbis. Liminality is the name for our collective experience during most of this passing century. In the future, patterns of wholeness surely will emerge from this presently deconstructed and dissolved mass of tradition, ideology, custom, and attitude. Based upon deep structures of archetypally anchored image and form, they eventually will gather energies and direct them into artistic, cultural, social, and religious structures we cannot yet foresee. From where we stand today, we can discern the past—the wrecked premodern and traditional patterns; the decades of de-structuring, warfare, and corrosive intellectual analysis; the free experimentation with lifestyle, marriage, family patterns, and sexuality that is inherent in deep liminality—but we cannot yet identify with certainty the emergent structures of new patterns of wholeness.

In this book, I shall not try to decipher this impending global development, which doubtless will take many decades to unfold and solidify. Rather I shall concentrate upon the notion of psychological transformation itself and upon the outcomes of transformation for the individual person. Transformation is by no means behind us. Individuals and collectives still are in the firm grip of powerful transformational forces, and this is sure to be the case into the foreseeable future. It is useful for us to understand the nature and purposes of individual psychological transformation, first, in order to manage the anxiety that attends it; and, second, to identify its significant features so as to differentiate transformation from simple deconstructive nihilism on the one side and from utopian delusion on the other. It is fatefully important that we begin to see individuals as indispensable wholes, rather than as cogs in a giant machine or grains of sand on the beach of collective humanity. Furthermore, there may be important analogies that can be drawn between individual transformation and collective processes of change. Once the individual's process is clarified, models can be created for examining collective processes as well.

What, then, are transforming persons? And what do they look like? Transforming persons are not necessarily ideal people who elicit our admiration and call for emulation. They are people who are in the process of transformation and therefore often are incomplete, like works in progress. They are becoming themselves, yet they are also, oddly, becoming what they have not yet been. Often they are people who transform others and their surrounding cultures. It is my personal conviction that only those who have been or are being transformed can be agents of further transformation.

In this book's four chapters, I want to consider several factors attendant upon the full emergence of the self in adulthood. In chapter 1, I describe the process of transformation in adulthood and what it is like to be deeply affected by it. I go on, in chapter 2, to consider the means by which psychological transformation comes about in people: the transformative image. In chapter 3, I look at the role of intimate relationships in transformation. And in chapter 4, I study and compare Rembrandt's and Picasso's self-portraits and Jung's architectural statement at Bollingen, with the aim of describing, through the use of these figures as examples, some of the characteristic features of transforming persons.

My guiding idea throughout this work is the notion that transformation leads people to become more deeply and completely who they are and have always potentially been. Change to the new, paradoxically, is change to the very old. Transformation is realization, revelation, and emergence, not self-improvement, change for the better, or becoming a more ideal person. The transforming person is someone who realizes the inherent self to the maximum extent possible and in turn influences others to do the same.

Transformation

Prologue

One day in late November, while I was taking a walk along a well-traveled road in the hills of North Carolina, my eye happened to fall upon a chubby caterpillar busily schrooching along and hurrying down the side of the road. I paused to watch its progress, as over the next thirty minutes it pushed along the gravel road for a considerable distance. The sun was still warm in the autumn sky, and it raised some sweat on my skin as I stood and watched and slowly followed the progress of the determined creature.

I had time to wonder what the caterpillar was thinking. I guessed that it was heading for a sheltered place in which it would spin its cocoon and begin pupation. The place must be safe from predators and protected against wind and storms. I wondered if the caterpillar thought about what was going to happen. It was intent on getting somewhere, doing something and doing it urgently, but did it know what it was in for? Did it have a vision? Can a caterpillar dream of flying?

The questions piled up and went unanswered. After we had traveled about a hundred yards together, the caterpillar crawled into a thicket of brambles and bushes that grew along a low wooden fence, and I lost sight of it. It must have found a place to spin its threads and go into suspended animation for a week or a season. If it was lucky and survived the ordeal, it would become a magical winged creature. It would emerge as a totally different kind of being, a butterfly, no longer committed to the earth but instead hovering above flowers and darting from blossom to blossom, following the flow of air and its own intuition. It would have freed itself from the confinement of a tomblike cocoon, dried its wings, and found the talent to soar.

CHAPTER 1

Emergence of the Self Imago in Adulthood

The driving force, so far as it is possible for us to grasp it, seems to be in essence only an urge towards self-realization.

—C. G. Jung

A thirty-five-year-old woman once came to my office to discuss some recent dreams. To my astonishment, and also my everlasting gratitude, she told me a dream of such profound transformation that I never have forgotten it.

I am walking along a road, feeling depressed. Suddenly I stumble on a gravestone and look down to see my own name on it. At first I am shocked, but then strangely relieved. I find myself trying to get the corpse out of the coffin but realize that I am the corpse. It is becoming more and more difficult to hold myself together because there is nothing left to keep the body together anymore.

I go through the bottom of the coffin and enter a long dark tunnel. I continue until I come to a small, very low door. I knock. An extremely old man appears and says: "So you have finally come." (I notice he is carrying a staff with two snakes entwined around it, facing one another.) Quietly but purposefully he brings out yards and yards of Egyptian linen and wraps me from head to foot in it, so I look like a mummy. Then he hangs me upside down from one of many hooks on the low ceiling and says, "You must be patient, it's going to take a long time."

Inside the cocoon it's dark, and I can't see anything that is happening. At first, my bones hold together, but later I feel them coming apart. Then everything turns liquid. I know that the old man has put one snake in at the top and one at the bottom, and they are moving from top to bottom, and back and forth from side to side, making figure eights.

Meanwhile, I see the old man sitting at a window, looking out on the seasons as they pass. I see winter come and go; then spring, summer, fall, and winter again. Many seasons go by. In the room there is nothing but me in this cocoon with the snakes, the old man, and the window open to the seasons.

Finally the old man unwraps the cocoon. There is a wet butterfly. I ask, "Is it very big or is it small?"

"Both," he answers. "Now we must go to the sun room to dry you out."

We go to a large room with a big circle cut out of the top. I lie on the circle of light under this to dry out, while the old man watches over the process. He tells me that I am not to think of the past or the future but "just be there and be still."

Finally he leads me to the door and says, "When you leave you can go in all four directions, but you are to live in the middle."

Now the butterfly flies up into the air. Then it descends to the earth and comes down on a dirt road. Gradually it takes on the head and body of a woman, and the butterfly is absorbed, and I can feel it inside my chest.[1]

The kind of developmental unfolding imaged in this dream and in its central metaphor, the butterfly's metamorphosis, is what I want to explore in this chapter. This is a transformational epoch that extends over a considerable period of time, over years or even a decade or more, during which people find themselves living in a sort of limbo. I call this *liminality.* The very foundations of a person's world are under construction during this time. Such transformation is life-changing. It is a massive reorganization of attitude, behavior, and sense of meaning. While this typically is triggered by a singular encounter with a transformative image—a religious symbol, a dream, an impressive person, an active imagination—or by major life trauma like a divorce, the death of a child, or the loss of a parent or loved one, it will take months and years to become complete. When there is such a major passage, one can think in terms of metamorphosis or transformation, the passing over (*meta-, trans-*) from one form (*morph-, forma*) to another. Sometimes the changes and shifts of attitude are subtle while they are happening, and one is hard-pressed to know what if anything is going on. In the long run, though, the change turns out to be lasting and profound.

That people change and develop significantly in the course of their whole lives seems to us today a commonplace observation. We take it for granted that there are "stages of life," "life crises," and "developmental phases." It was not always so, but now these are part of the contemporary vocabulary and its clichés. Twentieth-century psychology has contributed a great deal to this vision of human life. Hundreds of studies have been dedicated to exploring and describing human psychological development, beginning in earliest infancy and proceeding through adolescence and adulthood to old age. Many accounts now exist outlining various emotional, cognitive, moral, and spiritual dimensions of this development. The psychological life of people now is seen as changing and developing almost endlessly.

At the beginning of the century, Freud found only four stages of psychosexual character development worth discussing, and all of these occurred in early childhood. He would have frozen major character development at the end of the oedipal stage (roughly ages four to six), and he considered the rest of life as fundamentally only a repetition of these early patterns. Jung soon disagreed. To begin with, he argued for a pre-sexual stage (with the focus on nourishment), followed by preliminary sexual stages that unfolded in childhood and reached maturity in adolescence.[2] He later expanded upon this by proposing a full lifespan developmental schema divided into two major parts: the first half of life, which has to do with physical maturation and social adaptation; and the second half, which is governed by spiritual and cultural development and aims. Other theorists, Erik Erikson among them, have argued that people pass through a discrete number of stages. Erikson proposed eight clear-cut and discernible major phases of development that can lead to one of any number of results in the unfolding epigenetic progression.[3] Each phase is loaded with its own specific tasks, hazards, and outcomes. However one divides it, whether more pessimistically as Freud did or more optimistically as Jung and later theorists of the psyche have, the human lifespan has been conceptualized in this century as encompassing several psychological phases, each passage between phases entailing a period of crisis.

A central question I will be focusing on in this book is: After childhood and youth, what? What happens to people developmentally after they have put childhood behind them? Some, of course, would argue that this never happens. This book is dedicated to the opposite view. I believe that most people grow up and become more whole and complete than their (demonstrable) repetitions can possibly account for in any significant or interesting way. But my thesis is not, on the other hand, that there is a vast smorgasbord of options, or changes bordering on the endless, like the image of the "Protean self" that has been proposed by Robert Jay Lifton. There may be a plethora of changes and alterations in personality and character—the so-called "stages of development"—but, following Jung, I hold that there are two great developmental eras, a first and a second half of life. The first is a growing and adaptational era, and the second is a consolidating and deepening era. While important psychological developments take place during infancy and childhood, for me the most interesting and spiritually significant ones happen in adulthood, at midlife and after. I do not believe that identity forms, in any deeply significant way, until after midlife, typically in a person's late forties. This identity is rooted in what Jung called the *self,* rather than in the earlier psychosocial structures that have been assumed for the sake of adjustment and adaptation.

I do not mean to imply that we can become whatever we want to be, our ideal self. This is a typical illusion of the first half of life, perhaps one important and necessary for installing sufficient ambition and self-confidence in a youth to make the great effort needed for adaptation. But limits are placed on our psyches just as they are on our bodies. Ideals may be no more attainable in psychological life than they are in the physical arena. We may want to be like Michael Jordan physically, but only a few will even begin to approximate his athletic form. In our Western religious traditions, there has been an emphasis on becoming Godlike through an *imitatio Dei* or *imitatio Christi*. This may be no more attainable than becoming small versions of Michael by imitating his moves on the basketball court. When we look at people's lives empirically, we usually see a picture entirely different from what these individuals want to be like or want to appear to others to be. If people live long enough, they become themselves, which is not always reckoned as ideal; they may even be shunned and despised. The self is not something we select; we are selected by it.

What I am interested in exploring is what actually happens to people inwardly when childhood, with its well-known "stages" and its scars and complex formations, is completed and outgrown, not only chronologically but psychologically. What are the instrument and the design that shape our ends, if not childhood patterns and adolescent "outcomes"? Does another kind of psychological development begin in adulthood? If a person stops looking back to childhood with regrets and secret longings for an ideal paradise, or back to post-adolescence with surges of desire for eternal youth and ever greater expansion of ego and mastery of the world, as well as the physical perfection denied the aging—and must we not all finally do this?—is there then an opportunity for a second birth, another beginning?

I believe that there is such an opportunity and that this starts around midlife, or sometime in adulthood after its first phase has ended. Sometimes this development begins rather early—in a person's early thirties, for instance. Classically it takes place around forty. Occasionally it is delayed until a person has reached the mid-forties or even the early fifties. At some point, though, a second complete era of psychological and spiritual transformation gets under way, similar to what happened in adolescence but showing different psychological contents and meanings. While the new developments build on and make use of the old structures, they also transcend them.

In terms of lifespan development and cycles, I propose the following schema. Childhood (a first caterpillar stage) culminates in a metamorphosis during adolescence, when adult sexuality enters the biological and psychological picture. This leads to a new psychosocial identity (a *persona*), which Erik Erikson outlines very well in his works on adolescence, and to the establishment of an adultlike person whose true self is, however, still latent and hidden by the adaptive structures and requirements of this stage of life. This is a second caterpillar stage. It culminates in the midlife metamorphosis, which gives birth to the *true self,* and this personality becomes filled out and actualized in the second half of life. It is possible that there is a third caterpillar stage between midlife and old age, when there is yet another transformation. This final metamorphosis typically gives birth to a sense of self that is highly spiritual and oriented toward the timeless, as a person prepares for the final letting go and what may be a fourth transformation, physical death. In this book I will be discussing primarily the second transformation—midlife and the following period that reaches to old age—but in the examples I cite in the fourth chapter, there is also consideration of the third transformation in old age.

Before using the butterfly metaphor to extend our thinking about human psychological transformation in adulthood, I want to say a word in defense of analogical thinking. For some people this is a highly dubious intellectual undertaking. Those who prefer abstract and mathematical, or purely logical, thinking often warn about the dangers of using metaphor and analogy. Metaphors can mislead us into making foolish mistakes, they argue—quite rightly. Look at the alchemists, for example, chasing their fantasies of turning base metals into gold. Chemistry could not become a true science until practitioners of this laboratory sport gave up their dungeons and dragons. So the argument goes. Watch those metaphors! This line of thinking certainly is correct in many respects, especially with regard to unconscious metaphors that trap thinking in concrete.

Ultimately, however, this position also leads to sterility and obsessiveness. Nor does it apply to all areas of knowing. Metaphors can help us to think our way into new territory. They can provoke reflection and suggest new avenues. In fact, it is impossible to think without them. Look at the phrase "new avenues" in the previous sentence. A metaphor is used there to compare thought processes and streets. It is useful, not misleading. The images of a metaphor can extend our range of thinking and suggest new applications of old learnings and behaviors. Philosophers Lakoff and Johnson have argued in their book, *Metaphors We Live By*, that metaphors are essential in concept building. The use of metaphor is woven into the very fabric of the thought process itself and is fundamental to it. Ordinary language is larded with metaphors, and it is impossible to communicate without them. In fact, our notions of reality are made up largely of metaphor. "Our ordinary conceptual system, in terms of which we both think and act, is fundamentally metaphorical in nature,"[4] Lakoff and Johnson assert. This does not mean that metaphors cannot be misleading, but it does mean that we cannot get away from them. And as these authors convincingly show, metaphors are necessary if we are to have concepts at all.

A butterfly's metamorphosis from larva to pupa to adult is a useful metaphor for the human psychological process of transformation in adulthood. This is an image that I want to press further. How far can it carry our thinking about the process of psychological transformation?

Butterflies undergo what is called a complete metamorphosis. However, they also pass through a long series of preliminary moltings before they arrive at the complete metamorphosis. This distinction between large and small transformations will be useful in thinking about psychological transformations in people. Suppose that we undergo many little ones and then, at midlife, a big one. This may suggest a useful perspective on the multitude of changes that occur in the course of a whole lifetime.

When larvae hatch from their eggs, they begin immediately to feed, typically on the leaves of the plant where their mothers laid the eggs. From then on they eat without ceasing, and, as they grow to be many times their original size, they shed their skins in a series of moltings. While the moltings are lesser metamorphoses, in themselves they also constitute crises. During each molting, the larva is left vulnerable until a new protective coat grows around it. (Emotional vulnerability and nakedness are characteristic of change periods in a person's life. In fact, this may be the most evident sign of imminent transformation.) When the caterpillar finally is fully grown, its body chemistry changes. What had been a stable balance between the molting hormone and the juvenile hormone suddenly shifts in favor of the former, and this induces pupation, a massive molting rather than just another simple one. The hormone that prevents premature pupation has been termed a youth hormone or a rejuvenation hormone. It is secreted by the *corpora allata,* the "juvenile glands," and it acts as a brake on what otherwise would be a rush to the butterfly stage. It is only when the hormones of the prothoracic gland gain the upper hand, as a result of a process of diminishing levels of the juvenile hormone in the bloodstream, that metamorphosis is triggered. (The promise this hormone holds for eternal youthfulness, not surprisingly, has stimulated efforts to isolate it and use it to realize the common human fantasy of remaining forever young and beautiful. If we could just get enough of this hormone into our systems, perhaps we would never age!)

Think back to the dream of transformation recounted at the beginning of this chapter. The dreamer, who was thirty-five years old at the time of the dream, had reached her full physical and social maturity as a woman. The first half of her life was coming to an end. Until then she had lived on schedule, so to speak, accepting tasks and roles laid down by culture and nature. The various steps of maturation, physical and psychological, had been traversed. She had made good use of her native talents and advantages in life to adapt to the social setting into which she had been born. She had developed a highly effective social persona and had achieved a suitable psychosocial identity; she had realized her female biological potential for childbearing; she was in a favorable position educationally and economically. She had lived the first half of life well enough, and she had accomplished its primary objective—adaptation to the physical and cultural world into which she was born. Ego development, while not ideal, at least was more than adequate. Now, at the midpoint of her life, she was experiencing a "hormonal shift" (metaphorically speaking—she was not yet in menopause), and it registered as depression:[5] "I am walking down a road, feeling depressed." Her actual life in fact was no longer satisfying, and indeed she was threatened with a major depression. The stage of adult caterpillar life was about to end, and unconsciously another phase was in preparation.

Today a depressed person can take Prozac to correct the mood. But imagine what would happen if the caterpillar went to an insect psychiatrist and asked for a prescription of antidepressants to fend off emotional pain: "Moltings have become so hard lately. I'm just beside myself during those painful periods! Help me!" If the doctor were not aware of the bigger picture—of the nature of the life cycle and the importance of bearing the suffering at this particular juncture—the big crisis might be postponed by drugs. Medication, as useful as it sometimes may be for reducing psychic pain, is by no means always the answer. Pupation is terrifying, but without it, there is no transformation, no butterfly. A shift in chemistry is needed for the next stage to begin. The juvenile hormone puts off pupation until the larva is able to take on a full metamorphosis. Delay is a necessary defense against too early onset of maturational processes. One can look at maturation as an increasing ability to bear what at times is the overwhelming challenge of major transformation, with its extreme anxiety and depression. Earlier crises are practice for the later ones which inaugurate the second half of life and later end that life.

Some budding adolescents resist the normal physical developments that accompany another critical stage of development. Anorexia nervosa in adolescent girls, for instance, often is rooted in the wish to remain presexual, to cling to childhood. The same dynamic holds in midlife. Resistance to transformation is strong. If one extends the reasonable wish to be youthful too long and continues to get pumped up with juvenile hormones beyond the appropriate time, however, one will become nothing more than a slowly aging caterpillar, struggling ever harder to put off the final day of reckoning. The mature personality and the deeper, archetypally based identity will not form. After a certain point in life, the *puer aeternus*[6] (eternal adolescent) and his sister, the *puella aeterna,* cut rather sorry figures, precisely because they lack this quality. It is a quality of depth and integrity, rooted in layers of the psyche beyond the superficial levels of social adjustment (*persona* formation) based upon a need to please, to join in, and to get along. Cosmetic surgery may prop up the illusion of never aging, while the real benefit of aging—transformation into one's full identity as an adult person—is lost in the cuttings on the floor. The shift in body image and chemistry is part of the whole life plan, not an increasing deficiency to be remedied artificially so as to feel young a while longer.

When the caterpillar hears the call, it begins preparing for pupation. The change that now transforms the caterpillar into a pupa is of far greater magnitude than any other molts it has undergone previously. This is the big one. Entirely new structures will emerge and become dominant as a result of this metamorphosis. Complete metamorphosis is a dramatic transformation, out of which a creature emerges that bears no resemblance to the one that existed before. Who would guess, just by looking at it, that a swiftly darting butterfly once was a thick worm lumbering heavily along the ground? How does this happen?

First of all, this actually is the same creature. Only in appearance is it utterly different. At a deeper level, it carries what were formerly latent structures, now made vibrantly manifest, along into this new stage of life. The form has changed, but it is not a different being, not a changed soul. Scientific observers have determined that the rudiments of both pupal and adult structures already are present in the mature caterpillar. Indeed, some of these rudimentary structures are present at the cellular level during early embryonic development in the egg. They are primal and always have been part of the organism, but before this phase of life they remained latent. In their latent form, they are called "imaginal disks,"[7] a name that indicates their status as faint images or prefigurations rather than as substantial organic structures. It seems that these disks simply bide their time until conditions are ready to support their advancement into mature form in the adult. The adult insect must develop in its own time, and when it does, its form is called the *imago*.[8] The butterfly is the imago of the insect that previously was incarnated as a caterpillar. The passage from imaginal disks to imago is, as we shall see, a difficult and sometimes hazardous process.

In passing from one form to another, the butterfly draws upon the latent structures that have been present all along but were undeveloped, hidden from view, or disguised by other features. The change from caterpillar to butterfly is a transformation in which underlying latent structures come to the surface and assume leading positions, while other features that were prominent change radically or disappear. In this, we recognize an important feature of psychological transformation in human adults. If one looks carefully into an adult person's early life, into infancy and childhood traits and fantasies and early dreams—that is, into the substructures latent and unconscious in earlier stages of life—one usually can find rudimentary and partially formed images of things to come. The child is father to the man, the old expression goes. In childhood and adolescence, attitudes take form which later will undergo change and development but which will, for all that, express themselves as variations on the same theme.

Character structure, psychological typology, interests like sports or music, sexual orientation, vocational inclination, vocal cadences, sense of humor—all of these may take shape early in life and be recognizable in the adult who grows out of the adolescent, even if they are subtly altered and readjusted in light of later experience. Sometimes the later features that become so prominent in the adult are, like imaginal disks, tucked away behind more obvious features and gross behaviors. In the lives I will be considering later in this work—those of Rilke, Jung, Rembrandt, Picasso—we shall see that some qualities that are largely hidden earlier in life become the most prominent and outstanding features of the second half of life. This can be, and indeed has been, conceived of as the difference between the "false self" of persona adaptation in childhood and early adulthood and the "true self" that emerges after midlife. The socially adapted personality often hides in the shadows personality elements that are the "stone that the builder rejected" and later become the cornerstone of the adult personality. These might be prefigured in the youthful personality but are hard to identify except in a careful retrospective analysis.

The early indications of these later structures, before the full structures show themselves more clearly later in life, could be subject to a variety of interpretations. In the early stages of development, one could imagine a thousand possible outcomes. Only in retrospect can one see the full imago that previously was hidden in shadow. The future is prepared in the womb of the past and the present. For some people, there seem to be huge discontinuities in life—almost several different lifetimes—but this is only a surface phenomenon. At a deeper level, there is a single process of becoming; major but perhaps hidden continuities exist between latent structures from the past and prominent structures of the present. Children sometimes will dream or imagine or play-act their future imagos with surprising intuitive accuracy.[9] One may be bold enough to think that a psychological ground plan for life is present all along and that, if occasionally we contact it in dream or intuition or vision, we can foresee the future of our lives.

The stunning transformation of caterpillars into butterflies through the virtual death of pupation historically has given rise to much speculation about analogies to human fate and destiny. Perhaps, it has been proposed countless times, our entire earthly life is analogous to the caterpillar stage. Our physical body is a larva. At death, when the body begins to decay and dissolve into its basic chemical elements, a soul emerges from it, like the butterfly from a pupa, and soars into a life beyond the material world. The butterfly, so this thought goes, symbolizes our immortal soul, which is released by death from the larval body and freed into its new life in the spirit. The physical experience of dying is really only a kind of pupation. This analogy between the immortal soul and the butterfly is ancient and widespread. The Homeric Greeks saw the soul leaving the dead body as a butterfly, and the Aztecs considered the butterflies flut-

tering in the meadows of Mexico to be reborn souls of fallen war-
riors. The Balubas and Luluas of Kasai in Central Zaire speak of the
grave as a cocoon from which a person's soul emerges as a butterfly.
Turkic tribes in Central Asia believe that the dead return in the form
of moths.[10]

In our skeptical scientific culture, we are inclined to doubt the
possibility of an afterlife, so we look for transformation on this side
of the grave. It is this skeptical attitude, I believe, that has opened the
way to observing (and expecting!) developmental changes in humans
during their earthly life. Only since the end of the Middle Ages has
there been a general awareness of such "stages of life" as childhood,
adolescence, adulthood, and old age. And it has only been in the
twentieth century that these stages have been observed carefully from
physical, psychological, and spiritual viewpoints. We prefer to locate
transformation on this side of the grave.

As depicted in the dream, the central act of the transformation
drama takes place during the pupa stage. This is when the larva dis-
integrates and gradually assumes the form of a butterfly. The onset
of pupation, which is the name of the process by which a caterpillar
enters its dark night of the soul, is triggered by a shift in hormonal
balances. This change in body chemistry stirs the larva to begin preparing for its virtual death and rebirth. The caterpillar stops feeding
for the first time and sets out to find a safe place to pupate. This does
not always mean that it will spin a cocoon. Some types of caterpillars
do not.

There are three main methods of pupation, only one of which
involves the construction of a cocoon. In one, the pupa hangs head
downward, attached by an organ called a *cremaster* that is deeply embedded in a mat of silk fibers secured to a stable surface such as a
fence post. The vulnerable pupa is protected by a hardened surrounding shell, and together they constitute the *chrysalis* (from the
Greek *chrusos*, "gold"; the *chrusallis* is a "gold-colored sheath"). In a
second group of insects, the pupa hangs by its tail in the open air,
held in place by a silk girdle that raises and supports its head. In a
third group, we find the true cocoon, which the larva creates by spinning silk and constructing a sac, often adding other materials to

make a firmer structure. While not all larvae create cocoons, all do go through a state of radical disintegration, so it is of paramount importance for them to find a safe place with adequate shelter. The quest for a suitable site may take considerable time and effort. Sometimes hours pass in a patient search for a place to settle. Once there, the larva goes to work spinning threads of sticky silk and anchoring them to a secure surface. A final expulsion of excreta frees the larva to begin building a cocoon; in the pupa there is no more excretion of waste.

Transformation of the larva into the mushy disintegrated pupa does not always occur immediately after entering into the cocoon. The larva can live intact inside the cocoon in a state of profound introversion for weeks or months, in what is called *diapause*. The duration of diapause is determined by the interplay of hormones secreted by glandular tissue in the head and prothorax. These hormones are carried by the blood to various parts of the body, where they trigger or inhibit specific activities. The pupal diapause ends, it is supposed, when the prothoracic glands, stimulated by a secretion of neurosecretory cells in the brain, release a triggering hormone into the bloodstream. These brain cells secrete their substances when certain environmental stimuli reach them. The necessary stimulus to set this chain of events in motion, for some species, is the increasing warmth of spring; for others, it is the moisture that indicates the end of a dry season. It is this combination of external stimuli and internal hormone release that determines the specific timing of pupation.

The endocrine mechanism of the insect has been compared by biologists to the function of the pituitary gland in vertebrates. There are organic tissue similarities, and both function as master timers of bodily activities. Adolf Portmann asserted in the early 1950s that the discovery of insects' brain chemistry and of the hormones that regulate the stages of an insect's life had been "one of the most significant achievements of zoology in the last fifteen to twenty years."[11]

This discovery further cemented the analogy between insect metamorphoses and human aging and transformation processes. Certainly human transformation also is biologically conditioned, and its timing has close links to sequences of physical growth and change. The turning point from first half to second half of life is timed by an internal biological clock, and the subtle physiological changes in hormonal balance and equilibrium that occur in humans at this stage of life may well be the key also to the timing of that profound shift in attitude, perception, valuing, and attribution of meaning at the psychological level that we call the midlife transformation. Hormones, in short, may be a key trigger of the midlife crisis. This means that the point of the life cycle that we call midlife is not only, or even primarily, a sociological phenomenon found only in Western postindustrial societies, as is sometimes supposed. It should be evident wherever and whenever people live long enough in a relatively healthy condition to experience this phase of life. When lifespans regularly and normally reach the seventies and eighties, the phenomena of midlife transition reasonably can be predicted.

Portmann, the prominent Swiss biologist and for many years a leading figure in the Eranos Conferences in Ascona, stressed the important insight that, while the hormones secreted by the larva are triggers for a process, they are in no way to be taken as creators of the content or the structures that come about through the processes they set off. They are stimulants that constellate a process which allows inherent potential to be realized. The innate potentials themselves "result from hereditary reaction patterns in the tissues." [12] They are created by genetic programs. In the case of human psychological transformation, similarly, it needs to be recognized that the hormonal changes at midlife do not account for the essential features of the new attitudes and for the content of the psychological and spiritual developments that come about. They do not create the images that transform consciousness (see chapter 2 for a discussion of these images), but they well may control the biological conditions under which the unconscious is stimulated to release these images into consciousness. Hormones can be the triggers of the psychic processes.

What happens when pupation finally comes into full play is a massive breakdown of larval tissue, called *histolysis*. ("At first, my bones held together, but later I felt them coming apart"—the dream.) While the disintegration of larval structures in the pupa is not total, there is a considerable amount of it (the most radical disintegration takes place in the muscular system). Histolysis is combined with another process that moves the now emergent imaginal disks into place and substitutes them for former structures. The most specialized larval structures give way to new specialized structures of the imago. Meanwhile the pupa exists in an impermeable, sealed integument ("he brings yards and yards of Egyptian linen and wraps me from head to foot"—the dream); the pupa has been described as "a complete introvert."[13] There is almost no exchange of substances with the environment and only minimal respiration by diffusion through the spiracles. There is no food intake and no discharge of waste.

This prolonged period of incubation and restructuring has captured the imagination of psychotherapists and other helping professionals who regularly accompany people through periods of transformation.[14] In my book *In MidLife,* I write about three phases of this process and refer to this one—the middle one—as *liminality.* It transpires "betwixt and between" the more fixed structures of normal life (the larva and imago stages). In liminality, a person feels at a loss for steady points of reference. When the established hierarchies of the past have dissolved and before new images and attitudes have emerged fully, and while those that have appeared are not yet solid and reliable, everything seems to be in flux. Dreams during this psychological metamorphosis tend to show themes both of breakdown (images of buildings being torn down, of changing houses, sometimes of actual dismemberment and physical disintegration) and of emergence (images of construction, giving birth, marriage, the divine child). Angst is the mood of liminality. A person is ambivalent and depressed, and this is punctuated by periods of enthusiasm, adventure, and experimentation. People go on living, but not quite in this world. The analyst feels like the old man in the dream quoted above—watching a process unfold, observing the seasons passing, waiting patiently for new structures to emerge and solidify. It is an article of faith that what is under way is "a system 'developing itself,' a process embodying the whole specific nature of the living creature"[15]—faith that a butterfly will emerge from the cocoon where liminality reigns.

Does the caterpillar know that it will emerge as a butterfly when it enters the cocoon, becomes a pupa, and dissolves? There must be an act of faith on the insect's part. "Instinct" is our bland name for a remarkable act of spontaneous courage. For the larva must not resist the process that grips it with such urgency, but must cooperate with all its energy and ingenuity. Some larvae, when they enter the stage of pupation, must perform amazing feats of gymnastics, "as though a man hanging by the grip of one gloved hand had to withdraw the hand from the glove and catch hold and hang from it, without using the other hand or anything else to hold on by during the withdrawal."[16] Surely the insect's resolve is accompanied by a guiding image, a sort of vision. As Portmann puts it, these "systems of action [the hormones] and reaction [the tissues] . . . are parts of a larger system, which already in the germ cell is attuned to transformation in time."[17] The insect has been waiting for this moment all its life. In metamorphosis, it is fulfilling its destiny by obeying the guidelines inherent in this "larger system." In analytical psychology, we refer to this master system as the *self*. The imago is programmed into the developmental agenda of the self. It is the fullest approximation of the self we will ever manifest.

Once the imago has taken shape within the pupal shell, the adult creature can emerge. At this stage it has a double task: first, to break out of the pupal encasement; and second, to free itself from the surrounding cocoon. For extricating itself from its protective covering, it either possesses cutters or is able to secrete a caustic substance that dissolves the cocoon. In one way or another, it is able to force separation from the protective shell. At a certain moment, the body forces a burst of fluid into the head and thorax, which puts enough pressure on the pupal shell to crack it open. Thrusting upward, the insect pushes its legs forward and then pulls its abdomen through the opening. Freed of encasement, it maneuvers itself to a place where it perches, wings downward, and begins to expand its body parts by swallowing large amounts of air into its stomach, or *crop,* and its tracheal sacs. At first it is a delicate and fragile creature with pliable structures. But muscular contractions force blood into the wing pads, which expand to their full size and begin hardening in place. The drying membranes of the body stiffen and hold the wings steady. They are now spread to their full extent. Other body parts also harden. Next the proboscis is formed by uniting the two jaws of the ancestral chewing mouth, forming a tube through which the butterfly can later draw liquids. Once formed, the tube is pushed neatly into place underneath the face. This is a rapid sequence of unfolding structures.

Compared to the lengthy period of pupation, which may have extended over weeks or months, or in some cases even years, the final emergence of the adult is lightning fast. It may take only fifteen minutes. Within so brief a time, the insect becomes ready to take up its adult life as a butterfly. The dream depicts the same process: there are intense periods of activity at the outset and at the conclusion, and a long spell of slow transformation in between. At the beginning is the sudden entry into pupation, as the hormonal balance shifts and depression sets in and an intense preparation is begun for what is to come. At the end there is the emergence of the new form, a butterfly, which, in the dream, after drying out and trying its wings, becomes the dreamer-as-human again, while the butterfly is absorbed into her center as a soul image. The butterfly is a symbol of her new nature. She now has her imago, her adult form. Through this transformation she indeed has become a new being, but a being whom she always fundamentally has been. For the imaginal disks—the latent form—have been resident in her psyche since the beginning of life. The soul is fundamental, and the imago is its incarnated form. It is absorbed, as it were, into her earlier body form and character structure, a new psychic constellation that will guide and orient her through the course of her future life.

What living the process of transformation yields is a new form of life, something different from what has preceded it. At the end of the process, we look for a new self-definition and identity distinct from that of the first half of life. This new imago rests upon, or surrounds, the former character structure and gives it new meaning. It is not that the personality is changed such that old friends would not recognize the person anymore. But there is a new inner center of value and direction. There is a new consciousness of soul. This appearance of the inner life in the midst of adulthood is what in traditional terms is called the creation of the spiritual person.

The actual person who dreamed of transformation into a butterfly lived her midlife transformation in part by returning to school and assuming a professional identity, in part by establishing some new personal relationships and changing old ones, but in greatest part by learning to trust her unconscious and live her deeply spiritual nature. She could connect to what Jung called "the transcendent function," the link between conscious and unconscious process. A new form of life emerges from this dynamic exchange, which includes some pieces of the past, discards others, draws out latent images and structures from the primal sea of potentials in the unconscious, and assembles the parts into a new imago for adulthood. This is the form that then is lived, deepened, and enriched throughout the remainder of the individual's life. I believe the dream states this process better than any sort of conceptual language could.

What actually, concretely happens to people as a result of passing through midlife transformations, of course, varies greatly, as we shall see in the following chapters. Basically, each becomes the unique individual personality he or she always potentially has been. As we shall see in the next chapter, Carl Jung became the "Jung" we know as the psychological sage of Zurich. The midlife transformation of an exact contemporary of Jung's, the poet Rainer Maria Rilke, on the other hand, is the story of the full emergence of a major poet, for it was during this time in his life that he wrote the *Duino Elegies,* his most important work. Although he was a poet of considerable fame and high repute before he composed the *Elegies,* it was through this labor that he evolved into the truly mature poet we honor today. In the *Elegies,* the earlier pieces of Rilke's work all came together and formed a coherent unity. In many obvious ways, his journey was different from that of Carl Jung (which I shall describe in the following chapters), just as his life as an itinerant artist bears little resemblance to that of the bourgeois Swiss psychologist Jung, yet the two men's paths exhibit surprisingly numerous parallels and similarities. Both truly were episodes of profound transformation, fulfilling primal patterns.

I view Rilke's life between the ages of thirty-six and forty-six as an example of psychological transformation at midlife, and I use the

analogy of the butterfly's metamorphosis as a model to help understand what was going on in Rilke's deeply introverted personality
during this time. Before examining Rilke's midlife metamorphosis,
however, I would like to draw attention to some surprising and instructive points of contact between his life as a whole and that of
Jung, to begin establishing a platform upon which to build the argument of the following chapters. I compare Rilke to Jung because
the latter's life and work constitute the major theoretical backbone
of this essay on transformation and on the full emergence of the self
imago in adulthood.

René Karl Wilhelm Johann Josef Maria Rilke was born in Prague,
the capital of Bohemia, shortly after midnight on December 4, 1875.
In the same year, on July 26, Carl Gustav Jung was born a few hundred miles away in Kesswil, a small village near Romanshorn on Lake
Constance, where Switzerland borders on Germany. Geographically
and temporally, their lives lie close together. Culturally this is also the
case. They shared German as a mother tongue, and both were born
and lived just outside the borders of Germany itself, in areas that
were dominated by German culture. Incidentally, both also became
fluent in other languages (Rilke remarkably so in French, Jung in
English). In their early years, they shared a cultural milieu: that of
Middle Europe at the turn of the century.

Both also had difficult childhoods, because of marital problems
between their parents. Rilke's parents, whose marriage already was in
decline when René was born, actually separated during his childhood
and lived apart for the remainder of their lives. Jung's parents stayed
together but were not well suited to each other temperamentally, and
this friction generated an atmosphere of tension and unhappiness in
the home. In both cases, too, the boys' births occurred after the death
of former siblings: Jung's brother Paul died two years before his birth,
and Rilke's birth was preceded by the death of a first-born sister.
Their mothers understandably were affected by these losses, and
Jung's mother suffered a major depression in his early years. Rilke
was an only child, Jung an only child until his sister was born nine
years later. Both had conflictual relationships with their mothers; the
fathers in both cases were more positive figures, if somewhat distant

and unsuitable for idealization and identification. Both boys hated school and suffered the torments of abuse from teachers and fellow students.

A profound sense of vocation also was common to both men. Rilke found his vocation as poet and writer while still a youth, perhaps as early as middle school; Jung discovered his near the end of medical school, as he was preparing for exams in psychiatry. Both certainly were most blessed with religious "musicality," a keen sensitivity to spiritual settings and objects. Both were tightly connected to conventional Christian religiosity through their families, although neither practiced it denominationally in adulthood. Rilke's mother, a fervently pious Roman Catholic, added the name Maria to the long list of rather pretentious names given her newborn son, because he was born near midnight, the time when tradition says Jesus was born, and on a Saturday, which was considered Virgin Mary's Day.[18] Jung was born into a Swiss Protestant parsonage, and he had six uncles and a grandfather who were ministers in this denomination. Religion dominated the early years of both men. Both later sought out older men of genius to idolize, learn from, and apprentice themselves to— Rilke to Rodin, Jung to Freud. Each man, moreover, was destined for greatness and had instinctive faith in his inner *daimon*.

In 1912, the thirty-seventh year in each man's life, both began a journey—a *katábasis* and a metamorphosis—that would lead to transformation and to the emergence of a full adult imago. For each, the years between ages thirty-seven and forty-seven were crucial years, years of pupation and incubation, out of which would hatch a magnificent imago. This transformation at midlife would forge a stable adult identity as well as bring into reality the creative work each man was born to actualize.

To be exact, it was on the stormy morning of January 20, 1912, that Rilke, while taking a walk outside the Duino Castle near Trieste and studying a letter from his lawyer that pertained to his impending divorce, suddenly stopped in his tracks when "it seemed that from the raging storm a voice had called to him."[19] What he heard was the line which became the opening of the First Elegy: "Who, if I cried out, would hear me among the angels' hierarchies?" ["Wer, wenn ich schriee, hörte mich denn aus der Engel Ordnungen?"] (*Duino Elegies* 1:1–2).[20]

Princess Marie von Thurn und Taxis-Hohenlohe, the owner of Duino Castle, said that Rilke stood listening for a moment: "Who came? . . . He knew it now: (the) God." ["Wer kam?. . . Er wusste es jetzt: der Gott."][21] Then he took the notebook he always carried and wrote down the words that had formed themselves. Putting aside the notebook, he finished his business with the letter, and later in the day returned to the beginning of this new poem. By evening he had completed the First Elegy. This he transcribed and immediately sent to Princess Marie, his friend and patron, who was spending those days in Vienna. In the weeks following the First Elegy, he completed another poem, the Second Elegy, plus fragments of what later would become the Third (completed in 1913), the Sixth, the Ninth, and the Tenth Elegies (completed in 1922).[22] From the first moment of inspiration, it seems, Rilke knew that this was to be his major work. Intuitively realizing that the process of incubation and birthing would be long and hard, he complained in a letter to Lou Andreas Salomé, "I am affected almost as badly by conception as I was before by sterility."[23] Yet he had a first glimmering vision of what might lie ahead, and this would give him the courage and faith to hold out.

I think of the emergence of the *Duino Elegies* as an artistic expression of what was taking place in Rilke's psyche during his midlife crisis. In other words, it is a psychological document as well as an immortal work of art. One almost could say that this poem corresponds to Rilke's soul because it so profoundly embodies the contents, the dynamics, and the structures of his inner life. It reveals the essence of the man and, most importantly, conveys his deep identification with the poet archetype. For in Rilke's case, we must recognize emphatically, the poet imago was not a mere social convention, a persona—a psychosocial structure, such as is described by Erik Erikson in his discussions of adolescence and youth—but the realization of a primal human form. The imago is grounded in the self archetype. It is psychic bedrock.

Rilke's pupation began on January 20, 1912, and it continued until a second period of intense creativity shook the poet to his psychic foundations in early 1922, when the imago suddenly became complete. During this period, Rilke actually refers to himself as a pupa, in a letter to Hans Reinhart dated Nov. 29, 1920: "As soon ask the pupa in the chrysalis to take an occasional walk, as expect me to make the slightest movement."[24] In January 1922, almost exactly ten years after the first announcement in the wind at Duino castle, Rilke entered into a period of nearly sleepless poetic creation that extended into February and left behind, as a monument to artistic enterprise and visionary exaltation, the completion of all ten *Duino Elegies,* as well as, remarkably, *The Sonnets to Orpheus,* a somewhat lesser companion work. After this intense labor, the butterfly was born and soared to meet the world.

Between two distant winters—January 1912 and January 1922—and through a period that, not unimportantly, included the First World War, Rilke endured the liminality of pupation. This was an inauspicious time, collectively, for poets. Environmental conditions did not favor the completion of Rilke's inner process. Following the first outburst of inspiration, there was silence, with only occasional murmuring of things yet to come—completion of the Third Elegy in 1913, the appearance of the Fourth in 1915. Mostly it was a time of anxious waiting, of searching for the right external conditions, of preparatory work in voluminous letter writing, love affairs, makeshift living. Some of this delay could be placed at the feet of Rilke's neurotic ego, but much of it could be attributed to outer circumstances. The war interrupted his creative life traumatically, by requiring him to join the ranks of the Austrian army for some six months until highly placed friends could spring him free to pass the remainder of the war as a civilian in Munich. He was also hurt emotionally by the war, because it revealed a dimension of evil and stupidity in human affairs that cultured people of the time were unprepared to assimilate. The times were depressing. In addition, the old social order, on which Rilke relied for his livelihood and patronage, was passing, as European culture itself entered a period of massive structural reorganization. It seemed that everything was awry during these years.

After the war, Rilke reluctantly accepted an invitation to give readings in Zurich. On June 11, 1919, intending to return shortly to

Munich, he crossed the border by train into Switzerland near Romanshorn, very close to Jung's birthplace. Rilke never had found Switzerland to his liking—he felt that the mountains were too dramatic, the country too much like a calendar photograph to be real, the people lacking in refinement and cultural sophistication. When finally he managed to bring himself to cross the border, however, he discovered a land that would become home to him for the rest of his life. The audiences were grateful and enthusiastic. Most importantly, some wealthy Swiss admirers offered him financial and social support, as well as, in several cases, abiding and committed friendship. Most notable among these were Nanny Wunderly-Volkart of Zurich and her brother Werner Reinhart of Winterthur. Not unaware of the importance of these offerings, Rilke accepted the proffered beneficence and found ways of extending his visa privileges—at some cost and difficulty, as is usual in Switzerland. Thus he managed to continue living in various Swiss locales until his death in 1926. His preferred area was the French-speaking part of the country, Geneva and the Valais.

If one views January 20, 1912, as the onset of pupation and the period following as an extended diapause, when the creative spirit lies mostly quiescent, wrapped in a cocoon and encased in an impervious pupal shell, then it follows that the diapause terminated shortly after Rilke found his final and by far his most preferred home, the simple tower named Château de Muzot, near Sierre in the Valais. In structure, the Château de Muzot is not unlike Jung's famous tower at Bollingen. (Coincidentally, Jung and Rilke found their towers' locations within a few short months of each other.) By the end of July, 1921, Rilke was able to move into Muzot, and he passed the fall in his typical ways of preparing for a poetic visitation—letter writing, arranging furniture, and waiting for the voice to speak of things more profound than ego consciousness could manufacture. By January, the passages were open; what erupted in the week of February 7–14, 1922, was a veritable gale-force wind of energy and inspiration. Never before and never again afterwards would the poet be so thoroughly possessed by the Muse as when the text of the remaining *Elegies* poured from his pen. It was a furious culmination after ten years of waiting, a feverish burst into consciousness of images and thoughts and of a vision that had been waiting for release.

I cannot hope to give a complete account of the contents of the *Duino Elegies* here. Many books, dissertations, and entire conferences have been devoted to this subject without exhausting their seemingly infinite complexity and depth. I will only select some themes and images which seem to me central in this work and which also pertain to my theme of psychological transformation. I will discuss, if only briefly, the images of the Laments, the Angel, and the Open, together with the themes of transformation and death. In the *Elegies,* these are woven together and deeply interconnected and, I believe, constitute the major thematic fabric of the work.

Why call one's major life work *Elegies*? This I wondered when I first began to study Rilke's masterpiece. Of course, there are formal traditional reasons for this, as literary commentators have argued. Goethe wrote some famous elegies, so perhaps this was the literary reason for Rilke's choice. But I was looking for a psychological reason. Then I discovered that a mood of elegiac nostalgia and mourning dominates Rilke's entire artistic life. Perhaps because he was born to a mother who recently had experienced the death of her only child, a little girl, Rilke had a lifelong sensitivity to what he called the "youthful dead." A tone of mourning all that lost potential, of intense grief giving way sometimes to intimations of immortality but sometimes simply to loss, characterizes much of the poetry throughout his career. In the *Duino Elegies,* we find the deepest and most complete expression of this tone. Rilke had an ability to mourn almost without ceasing. It is as though the elegy—not as a technical poetic form, but as a fundamental structure of feeling—were an imaginal disk carried in Rilke's unconscious from the moment of birth. In the *Duino Elegies,* he places this in the foreground. It occupies a central position; it is a privileged structure in his adult imago. It seems, too, that the act of mourning was the essential catalyst—the stimulating or triggering psychological "hormone"—for Rilke's poetic creativity. His entire poetic *oeuvre* is, in a sense, a monumental lament.

But lament is not the *telos,* or ultimate aim, of this poetry. That is reserved for transformation. Lament is the occasion, the necessary condition, for transformation. The awareness of the "youthful dead," the poet recognizes in the First Elegy, often is needed by the living to make spiritual progress. Grief also stimulates the birth of music and is the generative force behind poetry:

> *Finally, they no longer need us, the early departed,*
> *one weans oneself gently from earthliness, as one*
>   *mildly*
> *outgrows the breasts of the mother. But we, who need*
>   *such*
> *great mysteries, for whom out of mourning so often*
> *blissful progress arises—: would we be able, without*
>   *them, to be?*
> *Is the legend of no avail, how in the lament about*
>   *Linos*
> *daring first music once pierced through parched*
>   *numbness;*
> *how it was only in startled space, which an almost*
>   *divine youth*
> *had suddenly stepped from for ever, where emptiness*
>   *first entered*
> *that motion that sweeps us away now and comforts*
>   *and helps us.*

> *Schliesslich brauchen sie uns nicht mehr, die*
>   *Früheentrückten,*
> *man entwöhnt sich des Irdischen sanft, wie man den*
>   *Brüsten*
> *milde der Mutter entwächst. Aber wir, die so grosse*
> *Geheimnisse brauchen, denen aus Trauer so oft*
> *seliger Fortschritt entspringt—: könnten wir sein*
>   *ohne sie?*
> *Ist die Sage umsonst, dass einst in der Klage um*
>   *Linos*
> *wagende erste Musik dürre Erstarrung durchdrang;*

dass erst im erschrockenen Raum, dem ein beinah
   göttlicher Jüngling
plötzlich für immer enttrat, das Leere in jene
Schwingung geriet, die uns jetzt hinreisst und tröstet
   und hilft.

                                    (1:86–95)

Tragedy is generative, spiritually fertile.

Rilke mentions the Greek figure Linus in this passage. According to Boethian tradition, Linus was a young singer who dared to compete with Apollo and was killed by the jealous god. Another story—from Argos—has it that Linus was abandoned by his mother, raised by shepherds, and later torn to pieces by dogs. This time Apollo was outraged by the injustice and sent a plague upon Argos. To appease him, the Argives invented dirges, called *lini,* and sang them in honor of the fallen youth. From the anguish of grief and guilt, dirge music—"daring first music" (1:92)—arose. There are also obvious associations between Linus and Orpheus, another famous singer who was known for his elegiac grief work and who also was torn to pieces.

What Rilke is emphasizing here is the transformative power of mourning. From it, music and poetry arise, which in turn convey the presence, in the voice, of the soul. For Rilke, this doubtless was the case. Mourning had its early roots in his childhood, in the emotion surrounding his infant sister's death and in what must have been a load of guilt borne by mother and survivor son. In his first years, Rilke was dressed by his mother as a girl. Named René, frequently a girl's name (spelled Renee but pronounced the same), the young boy functioned as a replacement for his lost sister. (Rilke himself later changed his name to the more unambiguously masculine Rainer.[25])

Lamentation and grieving are central to the poem, as they are to the poet and to his creativity. Rilke personifies lamentation in the Tenth Elegy, which concludes the cycle. Here we are introduced to the mythic territory and the history of the Laments. This is entirely an inner landscape of feeling. Like Dante being guided through the inferno by Virgil, the reader is led through this territory by the poet.

First there is a gaudy carnival in the City of Pain, which is noted and passed by, and then we are escorted past the outskirts of town where reality begins to set in and where lovers are seen to embrace. We follow the progress of a young man who walks into the fields beyond the city's boundaries. This figure, it turns out, has fallen in love with a young Lament, and he is following her into her territory, the Land of the Laments. At one point the youth turns to leave but then is captivated by the words of an older Lament who tells him about their clan and its declining history: "We were rich at one time" ["Einst waren wir reich"] (10:61), she says. She guides him farther into what we must now assume is Rilke's most essential inner landscape, the hills and valleys of his soul:

> And she leads him with ease through the broad
>   landscape of the laments,
> shows him the pillars of temples or the debris
> from those castles where lament-princes once wisely
> ruled the land. Shows him the tall
> tear trees and fields of blossoming sorrow,
> (the living know of these only as gentle foliage);
> shows him sadness's animals, pasturing,—and
>   sometimes
> a bird startles and, flying low through their lifted
>   gaze, traces
> into the distance the image that letters its lonesome
>   cry.

> Und sie leitet ihn leicht durch die weite Landschaft
>   der Klagen,
> zeigt ihm die Säulen der Tempel oder die Trümmer
> jener Burgen, von wo Klage-Fürsten das Land
> einstens weise beherrscht. Zeigt ihm die hohen
> Tränenbäume und Felder blühender Wehmut,
> (Lebendige kennen sie nur als sanftes Blattwerk);
> zeigt ihm die Tiere der Trauer, weidend,—und
>   manchmal

schreckt ein Vogel und zieht, flach ihnen fliegend
   durchs Aufschaun,
weithin das schriftliche Bild seines vereinsamten
   Schreis.

(10:61–69)

Nostalgia and sadness fill the air. They advance to the graves of the elders, "the sibyls and warning-lords" ["den Sibyllen und Warn-Herrn"] (10:72), and arrive at a tomb that resembles the famous Egyptian Sphinx. They have entered a realm of death. This is the classic *katábasis*, a descent to the underworld. In this land, the youth is required to grow accustomed to "the new death-sense of hearing" ["das neue Totengehör"] (10:85–86) and to the new constellations of stars, "Stars of the grief-land" ["Die Sterne des Leidlands"] (10:88). The Lament names them: Rider, Staff, Garland of Fruit, Cradle, Road, the Burning Bush, Doll, and Window. And looking even further:

But in the southern sky, pure as inside
a blessed hand, the resplendently clear "M"
that means mothers. . . .—

Aber im südlichen Himmel, rein wie im Innern
einer gesegneten Hand, das klar erglänzende "M,"
das die Mütter bedeutet. . . . —

(10:93–95)

In invoking the Mothers, the guiding Lament shows the visitor the ultimate source of the inner cosmos. At this point in the poem (and in life), Rilke has completed his psychological journey downward to the *prima materia* in the archetypal unconscious, and there he can name the major constellations that have orchestrated his conscious life. Most of these stellar configurations are familiar to readers of his earlier works. They are the symbolic reference points that have oriented his imagination over the course of the previous decades, and now they are drawn together under a single celestial dome and anchored in their ultimate source, the Mothers. Here we witness a moment of extraordinary integration, as though imaginal disks are snapping into place and forming the wings that will carry the poet skyward.

The old Lament reveals another mystery as she points out the source of human energy itself, the "well-spring of joy" ["die Quelle der Freude"] (10:99). She informs him that "Among mankind it's a sustaining stream" ["Bei den Menschen ist sie ein tragender Strom"]—(10:102). Both the indomitable will that takes humans by force and "wrings them, bends them, twists them and swings them, flings them and catches them back" ["wringt sie, biegt sie, schlingt sie und schwingt sie, wirft sie und fängt sie zurück"] (5:4–6); and the power that discharges a "seething chaos" ["wallendes Chaos"] (3:30) and arouses "that hidden guilty river-god of the blood . . . the Lord of Desire" ["jenen verborgenen schuldigen Fluss-Gott des Bluts . . . dem Herren der Lust"] (3:2–4) have their single source here in the mythical land of the Laments. In this land of death—the collective unconscious—also lies the origin and well-spring of life.

The Land of the Laments is this poet's own native land. It is the source of his joy and libido and the landscape of his soul. To arrive here, he must undertake the journey inward, leave the distractions available in the City of Pain (represented graphically by Rilke in his only novel, *The Notebook of Malte Laurids Brigge,* which, published in 1910, was based on his years in Paris as a young man). The poet must forego the joys and consolations of love and enter the land of the dead. There he can see the deepest constellations, and music is born in the emptiness of this egoless state. In these passages, Rilke displays the most intimate workings of his soul, as well as his experience of contacting the poetic Muse. It is in this land that the poet finds his true self and realizes his imago.

Rilke realized his full adult imago in the form of the poet, but this imago was carefully guided to its fulfillment by the numinous presence of the Angel. The figure of the Angel is in some respects the equivalent in the *Duino Elegies* of the old Master in the dream, each being a transcendent and catalytic figure who presides over the process of transformation. The Angel is implicitly present in the opening line of the First Elegy—"Who, if I cried out, would hear me then, out of the orders of angels?" ["Wer, wenn ich schriee, hörte mich denn aus der Engel Ordnungen?"]. This is the line that arrived in Rilke's ear fully realized in the winds above Duino Castle. Throughout the poem, Rilke speaks his lament to the Angel, whom he simultaneously fears and approaches, as holy ones are both drawn to and fear the numinous presence of God. Angels, Rilke tells us, transcend the dichotomy of life and death; indeed, they "often go about without knowing if they're with the living or dead" ["Engel (sagt man) wüssten oft nicht, ob sie unter Lebenden gehn order Toten"] (1:82–83). The Angel is a "stronger existence" ["stärkeren Dasein"] (1:3) who terrifies; "Every angel strikes terror" ["Jeder Engel ist schrecklich"] (2:1), Rilke cries out in a famous line. Angels are beings who are utterly self-possessed and who avoid all attempts by humans to appropriate their image. They elude humans by "re-creating their own streamed-forth beauty, drawing it back into their own faces again" ["die die entströmte eigene Schönheit wiederschöpfen zurück in das eigene Antlitz"] (2:16–17). They are equivalent to Plato's ideas—the Beautiful, *tò Agathón* itself—and to Jung's archetypes per se. Rilke reacts to the Angel with ambivalence, on the one hand directing to the Angel his notes of lamentation and his prayers for comfort, while on the other confessing that "my call's always full of Away; you can't stride against current so strong" ["Denn mein Anruf ist immer voll Hinweg; wider so starke Strömung kannst du nicht schreiten"] (7:88–89). He is cautious about entertaining, in his mere humanity, the numinous presence of the Angel. People have been wounded by inviting angels too freely.

Yet the Angel also is the ideal and the goal of transformation. The angelic realm is pure invisibility, the symbolic achieved and realized. As the poet reflects upon the human condition, he places humanity between the animals, who are at home in the concrete world of objects and live at one with their instincts; and the angels, who exist in a realm of sheer transcendence. We humans, he writes, live in an "interpreted world" ["in der gedeuteten Welt"] (1:13), partly concrete and partly symbolic. Being neither altogether animal nor fully transcendent angel, humans are in transit, passing from one state to the other. This is the trajectory. And it is the task of humans, he says, to transform the concrete object world into the angelic order of invisibility:

> *Earth, isn't this what you want: to arise*
> invisible *within us?—Isn't your dream*
> *to be invisible once?—Earth! invisible!*
> *What, if not transformation, is your pressing*
> *assignment?*

> *Erde, ist es nicht dies, was du willst:* unsichtbar
> *in uns erstehn?—Ist es dein Traum nicht,*
> *einmal unsichtbar zu sein?—Erde! unsichtbar!*
> *Was, wenn Verwandlung nicht, ist dein drängender*
> *Auftrag?*

> *(9:67–70)*

Verwandlung (transformation), that signal word, appears significantly in this crucial passage. This is the poet's mission, which Rilke fully accepts: "Earth, my love, I will" ["Erde, du liebe, ich will"][26] (9:71). To me, this is the poem's most passionate moment. Here Rilke fully accepts his fate and imago as a poet, which means he embraces the business of transformation. He fulfills this vocation by transforming objects into language, by naming things—"house, bridge, fountain, gate, pitcher, fruit tree, window—at best: pillar, tower" ["Haus, Brücke, Brunnen, Tor, Krug, Obstbaum, Fenster—höchstens: Säule, Turm"] (9:33–36)—and then presenting them to the archetypal angelic orders with utmost intensity of feeling. Such is the poet's mission. This vocation is the Angel's gift to Rilke.

Transformation is Rilke's continuous meditation. He not only observes and intuits the angelic orders, but he addresses them with poetic offerings from the world of ego consciousness. Such naming toward the realm of the archetypes—a kind of communion—transforms concrete objects into words, sounds, and images, ultimately placing them into a matrix of transcendent meaning. This process has a remarkable parallel in the Roman Catholic rite of transubstantiation. The most common mundane objects of the creature world—in the Mass it is bread and wine, in Rilke's poetry it is house, pitcher, window, etc.—are transformed into sacred symbols with transcendent referents and properties. The poet is a priest who mediates between earthly concrete existence and heavenly transcendent Being. "There is in the first place a bringing to life of substances which are in themselves lifeless, and, in the second, a substantial alteration of them, a spiritualization, in accordance with the ancient conception of *pneuma* as a subtle material entity (the *corpus glorificationis*),"[27] Jung writes in his essay "Transformation Symbolism in the Mass." The same can be said for Rilke's poetic opus. He changes the mundane and inert into the transcendent and spiritual. A window is not only a window after the poet has named it with intensity. It is a *window*. He has induced a transformation from profane to sacred, from object to symbol. And this is what he does also with his own life. He lives the *life of a poet*.

In order to produce this magnificent opus, the *Duino Elegies*, Rilke had to suffer through the actual experience of his own transformation. Finally he was able to break into the Open, which for him is a term implying full realization of the imago. In the Open, butterflies can spread their wings and soar. It is the realm of complete freedom to be oneself in the deepest possible sense. To arrive at the Open, however, the poet must take one further step. He must journey *through* the land of the Laments and go on, alone. It is only through such radical isolation that this poet—a veritable pupa encased in a shell and enclosed in an impermeable cocoon—comes to his ultimate self-realization. He "climbs away, into the mountains of primeval grief" ["Einsam steigt er dahin, in die Berge des Ur-Leids"] (10:104), alone. In this radical gesture, he stimulates and awakens further images—in himself and in his readers—of empty cocoons and "rain that falls on dark soil in the spring" ["den Regen, der fällt auf dunkles Erdreich im Frühjahr"] (10:109). The poem ends with these words. The imago is complete, and the butterfly leaves its encasement. It is a time for freedom, the birth of the soul.

What we find at the conclusion of lengthy transformative experiences such as those of Rilke and Jung, who was undergoing his famous "confrontation with the unconscious" in precisely the same years, is a manifestation of the adult imago, the image of self that a specific individual is destined to realize in maturity after the caterpillar stage of childhood and youth is past. In one sense, as Jung repeats in his writings many times, individuation is never finished or completed, because there is always more unconscious potential to bring into the personality's full integration. Yet we must also conclude that an imago, once filled out after midlife has been traversed, shows the indelible outlines of the "whole person." What remains to be done in the second half of life is to deepen, to ripen, to add detail and substance to the image that has emerged. The life of the butterfly may be short or long, but from now on it will remain true to its achieved imago.

Rilke's life was cut short by leukemia. He died at the age of fifty-one, some four years after completing the *Duino Elegies*, his masterpiece. By the age of forty-seven, he had assumed fully the imago of an Orpheus, and he also had become the archetypal lyric poet for the twentieth century. Had Rilke lived another thirty years, as Jung did, he well might have written the equivalent of *Faust II* and become a second Goethe. Goethe is the archetypal poet for the Germans, as Orpheus is for the Greeks. As it was, with the creative energy remaining during his years of physical decline, Rilke wrote masterful, playful, much lighter, but delightfully provocative poems in his newly adopted language, French. He passed his last years in his beloved Château de Muzot, tending roses and receiving occasional visitors. It can be said that he completed his life, although he died at a relatively early age.

CHAPTER 2

The Transformative Image

*Many fathomless transformations of personality, like
sudden conversions and other far-reaching changes of
mind, originate in the attractive power of a collective
image.*

—C. G. Jung

"Listen to me," she said leaning forward. "I want to change. This is
not the person I want to be. This is not the person I AM!" She spoke
in a voice filled with passion and energy, the words bitten off in a
clipped and clearly enunciated accent.

"Can a person enter a second time into her mother's womb and
be born?" I asked. "How can I possibly help you? You are looking for
a miracle."

This conversation never took place in reality, but it has occurred
in my private thoughts many times during psychotherapy sessions. I
can see the urgent desire in the eyes, the need, the driving force behind the wish for transformation, and it is awesome. People want to
change. How can they do it?

On August 5, 1989, the *New York Times* carried an obituary of William Larimar Mellon, Jr. It caught my attention. Two half-columns
of print were juxtaposed with a picture that showed Mellon dressed
casually in an open-necked shirt, his hair a bit disheveled, squinting
through thick glasses, smiling slightly. A good-looking man, he appeared to be in his sixties when the picture was taken. The article

stated that Mr. Mellon had died at his home in Deschapelles, Haiti, at the age of seventy-nine. The writer made the point that William Mellon was a member of one of America's wealthiest families. Born in Pittsburgh, he had attended some fine schools and gone on to marry, divorce, and remarry. In the mid-1930s, he bought a ranch in Arizona and settled down to become a working rancher. When World War II broke out, he served in the OSS (the predecessor of the CIA) and was sent on missions to Portugal, Spain, and Switzerland.

The obituary does not say that Mellon met Jung in Switzerland, but it is likely. Jung was a close friend of Paul and Mary Mellon, relatives of William's, and Jung too was in contact with the OSS's network of spies operating under the direction of Allan Dulles, who was stationed in Switzerland during the war.

In 1947, Mellon happened to read an article in *Life* magazine about Albert Schweitzer, "the Alsatian medical missionary, philosopher and musician whose hospital at Lambaréné, in what is now Gabon, had become world famous."[1] Mellon became fascinated with Schweitzer's mission and wrote the doctor a letter asking how to set up such a hospital. Schweitzer sent back a handwritten letter advising Mellon about the need for medical training and addressing the practical problems involved in setting up a hospital under Third World conditions. From this letter, Mellon's life took its future direction. He enrolled in medical school and four years later became a physician. At the same time, his wife studied laboratory science. After graduation, they searched for a suitable country in which to build a hospital on the model of Schweitzer's Lambaréné. They settled on a site in Haiti that had been abandoned by the Standard Fruit Company, and in 1956 the Albert Schweitzer Hospital of Deschapelles opened its doors. Here Mellon and his wife spent the rest of their lives, working in the hospital and engaged in local community affairs.

If one asks how major changes like this come about in a person's adult life and looks for the means of such transformation, one quickly discovers the role of what I will be calling transformative images. For William Mellon, Albert Schweitzer was a transformative image. The image of Schweitzer's life and mission suggested and shaped the direction of Mellon's maturity. In this chapter, I want to discuss how these images work upon the psyche. The stories of Mellon and his wife—both healthy, affluent, successful adults who went through major transformations—offer evidence that such transformations actually do take place in the middle of life.

Transformative images are engaging and even arresting metaphors. To live through the transformational processes they often engender is a special experience. From the moment these images appear, they take possession of one's consciousness and, at least temporarily, change it, sometimes dramatically. Dream images, for example, sometimes will haunt a person for days and continue to draw out emotions and memories, incite desires, and even stimulate plans for the future. Occasionally a poem, a painting, a film, or a concert has the same effect. The major symbolic experiences of this kind we call religious. For a moment, one almost becomes another person; in the long run, one actually does. If these powerful archetypal images are strong and impressive enough, the whole fabric of a person's life can be transformed. Their effects are not only momentary. Over time they become irreversible. This is because these images reflect psychological content that is emerging in a person's life and give it shape. They are metaphors with profound underlying structural support and meaning.

If we look back at a life from its endpoint, rather than moving forward from its beginning in infancy and early childhood, we usually can find major eras and turning points laid out in stark relief. For those who cannot read a newspaper without studying the obituaries, this is a common perspective. Obituaries look back over a whole lifetime. They mark the end of a life and, if excellent, they indicate the most significant moments of transformation in the lives of their subjects. Written with scant detail and from an objective viewpoint, obituaries condense a life into a few features that define its essence, its major turning points, the crises and resolutions. They offer portraits and tell readers who these people were, at least in the eyes of the public. A short obituary can sum up an entire life in a few lines of spare prose. If the obituary is subtle, it also hints at the kind of spirit the individual embodied, the color and feeling tones of the person, the meaning this life had for others. It gives the reader a bird's-eye view of what perhaps had been a gradual process of unfolding development and achievement over the course of a lifetime, along with the sudden twists and turns that ended up defining its ultimate course.

An obituary nevertheless can only provide the merest hint of the complicated process involved in transformation. If we look more deeply into adult development through the encounter with powerful and compelling transformative images, what do we find? Perhaps more than any other psychologist before or since, Jung studied the phenomenon of transformation from the inside. Unlike the obituary writer, who must accept severe limitations in describing a person's life, being limited mostly to a view from the outside and from a public angle, Jung's vision focused on studying the inner world of the psyche. Jung viewed transformation as a profound process of change that takes place in the depths of the psyche. Sometimes it manifests itself only dimly in the outer features of a person's known life, however, and would not even show up in an obituary. It is a complex process with many possible outcomes, some of them judged as positive and some as negative.

In a key letter to Freud dated February 25, 1912, Jung wrote: "I have ventured to tackle the mother. So what is keeping me hidden is the *katábasis* [Greek: "descent," i.e., to the underworld] to the realm of the Mothers, where, as we know, Theseus and Peirithoos remained stuck, grown fast to the rocks."[2] At that moment, Jung was composing part 2 of his self-defining work, *Wandlungen und Symbole der Libido,* which would crystallize his distance from Freud into a permanent and irrevocable break and catapult him into his own midlife crisis. In 1912, Jung was thirty-seven. At this same age, William Mellon read about Albert Schweitzer in *Life* magazine. Jung was at the beginning of a personal crisis that would not be completely resolved until he was nearly fifty years old. The transformation that resulted from this crisis would set him on a course that, like Mellon, he would pursue to the end of his life. He would write about this profound shift theoretically and autobiographically for the rest of his days.

Jung broke with Freud for many reasons. Among them was a conviction that Freud overemphasized the role of sexual problems in the etiology of neurosis. As he got to know Freud closely during their years of collaboration—through many exchanges of letters, several visits to each other's homes, and traveling together by ship to America—Jung was struck by the older man's peculiar and intense reactions whenever they touched on the subject of sexuality. It was as if a god were summoned, Jung says in his late memoir. Freud's thought was dominated by this issue, and emotionally he was fixed upon it. To some this may have seemed like a magnificent obsession, but to Jung it did not make for good science. Jung was not uninterested in sex as a personal matter, but he really was not a devotee. His most powerful inner images were more philosophical than sexual. For him, libido could flow in the paths of sexuality rather freely and powerfully, as many writers have noted and even dwelt upon, but his fundamental personality constellation was organized by other images. Nevertheless, at this time Freud was his most important teacher—also a father figure and mentor—and when Jung broke with him, his emotional life entered a severe crisis. The latter coincided with his midlife years.

Until Richard Noll wrote his mischievous book, *The Jung Cult,* no one had highlighted the remarkable passage in the English Seminar of 1925 in which Jung tells about his transformation experience.[3] While Noll badly misinterprets this passage for his own tendentious purposes, he nevertheless performs a service in putting his finger on a central transformative image in Jung's middle years. In the seminar, Jung gave his students an account of his thinking and personal development to date, starting with the publication of *Wandlungen und Symbole der Libido* in 1911–12. Here he spoke publicly for the first (and, until his autobiography was published in 1961, the only) time on record about his inner experiences during the crucial period between 1912 and 1918, which in his autobiography he calls "Confrontation with the Unconscious." Much of what he said in the seminar also is reported in the memoir, but not the one experience in active imagination that Noll uses as the centerpiece for his contention that Jung saw himself as the messianic founder of a new cult. In fact, Jung used this personal confession not to declare some sort of messianic delusion, but rather to illustrate his point about psychological transformation. He was not out to make converts and followers. He spoke objectively, as though to a group of listeners interested in hearing about an exotic and moving experience he had undergone in a remote country. The experience he related had been transformative for him, and the image that remained in memory became a central reference point in his individuation process. Jung was speaking as a psychologist and reflecting on the inner side of transformation. This is different from what a biographer or obituary writer could provide, because such individuals typically are not privy to the private world of fantasy.

Jung told his audience how he first began doing active imagination in order to contact his unconscious fantasies. The first efforts were not successful, but then he broke through and came upon a group of figures: an old man who named himself Elijah, a blind young woman companion named Salome, and a black snake. This much also is recounted in the autobiography. What is not described there is the subsequent active imagination. Several days later, he tried again to contact these figures, according to the Seminar, but a conflict blocked the way. Two serpents, one white and the other dark, were fighting each other. Finally the black snake was defeated and left the scene. Jung now could go on. He next encountered the woman and the old man again, and eventually he entered a space that in the book he identifies as the underworld: "Elijah smiled and said, 'Why, it is just the same, above or below!'" It was the house of Salome and Elijah. Then comes the decisive event:

A most disagreeable thing happened. Salome became very interested in me, and she assumed that I could cure her blindness. She began to worship me. I said, "Why do you worship me?" She replied, "You are Christ." In spite of my objections she maintained this. I said, "This is madness," and became filled with skeptical resistance. Then I saw the snake approach me. She came close and began to encircle me and press me in her coils. The coils reached up to my heart. I realized as I struggled, that I had assumed the attitude of the Crucifixion. In the agony of the struggle, I sweated so profusely that the water flowed down on all sides of me. Then Salome rose, and she could see. While the snake was pressing me, I felt that my face had taken on the face of an animal of prey, a lion or a tiger.[4]

In the commentary that follows, Jung interprets these images by placing them in a symbolic context—which, Noll notwithstanding, obviously is where they belong. The text states: "When the images come to you and are not understood, you are in the society of the gods or, if you will, the lunatic society; you are no longer in human society."[5] This suggests that Jung fully realized the difference between fantasy and prophesy. At its core, he said, this experience in active imagination is equivalent to an ancient deification mystery, as practiced in religious circles such as the one at Eleusis. *The Golden Ass* of Apuleius, which contains an account of such a mystery, was well known to Jung. If a person's sanity is not sufficiently grounded in an ego that recognizes the difference between fantasy and reality, however, such a transformation of consciousness easily can result in delusions of grandeur, or worse. As a young psychiatrist at the Burghölzli Klinik in Zurich, where he trained and worked for ten years, Jung probably saw his share of such patients. He himself was not given to such delusions, fortunately, and was able to understand and assimilate the images on a psychological, interior level.

What Jung was demonstrating, drawing on his own personal experience, is the transforming power of imagination. The images that appeared in his active imaginings drew consciousness powerfully to themselves and had a transforming effect. In this instance, Jung changed form and became first a Christlike figure and then Aion, who, he explained, derives from the Persian deity Zrwanakarana, whose name means "the infinitely long duration."[6] Jung noted in his lecture that this process of deification formed part of most, if not all, ancient mystery religions. As Cornford puts it in a passage about the Greek mysteries at Eleusis, "So man becomes immortal in the divine sense."[7] In the presence of immortal archetypal images, a person takes on their qualities and features and spiritually is molded by them into a similarly immortal figure. This is a symbolic happening, but it shapes one's sense of identity and value. Aion is a god who rules over time, who controls the astrological sequences and presides over the calendar. "The animal face which I felt mine transformed into was the famous [Deus] Leontocephalus of the Mithraic Mysteries, the figure which is represented with a snake coiled around the man, the snake's head resting on the man's hand, and the face of the man that of a lion."[8] At this moment of transformation, Carl Jung became a classical image of deity. The experience would change him profoundly.

From the brief obituary of William Mellon, we cannot know what kinds of effect the image of Albert Schweitzer had on his inner life. Did he dream about Schweitzer, or have the equivalent of an active imagination with his image? He must have had fantasies about him, and at a deep level he identified with the image. From the evidence it is clear that Schweitzer became a compelling image for Mellon, one that changed his life beyond all recognition. One can only guess that, deep in the subterranean levels of Mellon's unconscious fantasy life, Schweitzer was a godlike figure whom he wished to emulate and with whom he identified, in a pattern much like Jung's experience in his active imagination with Christ and Aion. What Jung did through his method of active imagination was to unearth the unconscious fantasies and lift them up into the light of day, where they became the subject of his science. He shows us the inner side of the transformation process.

It seems clear from Jung's autobiography that active imagination became a kind of personal mystery religion for him. It is a method that offers a quasi-sacred space in which a modern person can encounter religious images and experience the spiritual effects that the mysteries provided for the ancients. The great discovery of this twentieth-century psychologist was that modern people—secular and alienated as they are from traditional customs and beliefs— nevertheless have access to the riches of all the great cultural and religious traditions. They can have a personal encounter with the archetypal images of the collective unconscious. Such images, if deeply engaged and regularly related to over a sufficient period of time, have the power to transform consciousness in the same way

*The Mithraic god Aion. Courtesy Biblioteca Apostolica
Vaticana Museo profano 7899.*

that traditional images and mysteries have transformed human awareness for millennia.

It is important, however, to point out a major difference between Jung's approach to these sacred archetypal images and traditional religious approaches. Jung strongly recommended letting oneself become affected by the images, even to the point of temporary identification with them. So far, he and traditional practices agree. However, Jung did not advocate remaining identified, whereas they do advocate this. Traditions want people to become as closely identified and united with the dogmatic images as possible, to practice *imitatio Dei*. Jung, on the other hand, disidentified and consciously reflected back upon the experience. He maintained a psychological distance from the archetypal images. It is this latter move that yields the individual. Otherwise the images, being collective, simply create replicas of themselves. Jung's notion of individuation is based upon a twofold movement: temporary identification with the unconscious images in order to make them conscious, then disidentification and reflection upon them as an individual. An individual is affected by the contact but does not become controlled or possessed by the images.

In his second active imagination, which Jung carefully noted as taking place in December 1913, his consciousness clearly was transformed—deified, if you will—by the images. The woman worships him and calls him Christ, the serpent twines around him, and his head becomes leonine. The images, too, change dramatically, particularly the image of Salome. Addressing him as Christ, she asks for healing. She is blind and would see. Jung declines the inflated status of Christ-the-healer, but he notes in passing that Salome is healed nonetheless. She receives her sight. So the archetypal image also is transformed—but only after Jung did sweat until water flowed down on all sides of him, he declares. He became the Crucified for a moment, and a miracle of healing took place.

Who is the blind Salome, and why is she blind? Jung himself identified her as "the inferior function which is surrounded by evil."[9] In *Memories, Dreams, Reflections,* he interprets her as a symbol of Eros and feeling.[10] It is well known that he considered himself to be an introverted thinking intuitive type, and therefore his inferior function was extroverted feeling. This is the function of relationship. There lie his *anima* (i.e., soul) and his blindness, and this is what prays to him for healing. Taken in this light, the conscious Carl Jung is the only one who *can* heal Salome, and she is correct to look to him to give her the miracle of sight. He must sweat it out on the cross of transformation in order to sacrifice his superior function— thinking—to give life and light to his undeveloped, inferior, blind feeling function, to obtain awareness of connection and attachment to others. Before he is deified as Aion, he is crucified as Carl the Christ, and his anima becomes more conscious.

Although I am focusing this discussion of transformative images on mature adulthood and the second half of life, I do not want to give the impression that archetypal images do not also shape and affect the young. On the contrary, they have extraordinary impact on the plastic psychic structures of young people. They are present *in potentia* from the beginning of life and may be constellated well before midlife arrives.

An example of how such an archetypal image can perform its coordinating and directive function in a young person appeared on my doorstep one summer evening. The doorbell rang shortly after dinner, and, when I answered, a young man about twenty years old explained that he was collecting donations for a group dedicated to saving the planet from ecological catastrophe. Its mission was to save the earth. I stepped outside and asked him to tell me about his organization and his involvement in it. I usually am not an easy touch for money, and I pressed this young man to justify his mission. Why was he concerned about the planet? What did his organization realistically expect to accomplish? Where would my donation end up—in his pocket? He was patient and answered my somewhat rude questions politely. He seemed clearly to be college material, intelligent, of good family. He was doing this, he said, out of conviction. He received little pay and no power or fame, and he was working strictly for the cause. Finally his voice broke a little; his hands pointed outward and swept across the landscape as he exclaimed, almost in tears, "Don't you see? Mother Earth needs our help! She is suffering!"

Now I understood. He was moved by an image of the Great Mother, and he was offering his energies in service to Her. A glimpse into the primordial world of archetypal images had galvanized his psyche and sent him on a mission. His psychic energy was being shaped and organized by this archetypal image and its implications. As the Great Mother, Earth was not just a disguised version of his personal mother ("My mother needs help"). This young man's passion was not Oedipal. He was moved by an age-old image of the Great Mother that has shaped and stirred human psyches from time immemorial. It is an image of Beauty (Plato), the Mother archetype (Jung); and its effect is to transform consciousness. Every nonpathological human psyche, if it is developed and realized above the base level of sheer survival and instinct gratification, is shaped by such images that orient life and give meaning to it.

The defining theoretical issue between Jung and Freud was precisely the issue of transformation. Freud was immovable on the subject. Adamant that psychological life was largely reducible to sexuality and that the sex drive supplies all the energy at the disposal of the psyche, Freud assigned all forms of human creativity and every kind of pleasure to the sexual realm. Moreover, he attributed all forms of neurosis and even psychotic disorders to causes that were rooted in distorted sexuality. This would mean, as Jung pointed out incredulously, that all cultural objects, including art, philosophy, religion, and commerce, were but pale substitutes for the real goal of human desire, namely sexual pleasure. All ideals would be mere disguises for frustrated sexual wishes, and all psychopathology would be laid at the feet of disturbed sexual functioning. Freud stubbornly held all this to be true, arguing that, in fact, human culture was the sham product of a complicated network of sexual compromises. *Sublimation* was his term for the process that fed the sex drive into the cultural act.

Jung could not believe that Beethoven's symphonies and the cathedral at Chartres could be explained as a sublimation of their creators' sexual instincts. Nor would he reduce Albert Schweitzer's thought, vision, energy, and missionary zeal to sublimated sexuality.

Jung would take the position that, if human beings do not manage to integrate their various instincts and drives through a transformative image, they will tend to drift into psychopathology; and psychopathology can prevent people from integrating psychologically around a transformative image. People who fail to coalesce in this way remain partial, in pieces, unintegrated. It is indeed a psychological tragedy if a person's psyche will not allow for integration around a transformative image. Borderline personality disorder is a case in point. Such an individual's deep conflicts and splitting defenses are so severe and entrenched that they destroy every attempt on the part of the psyche at integration. They smash potentially transformative images with the destructive force of intemperate rage and an anxiety that borders on panic.

First, though, the question was how to account for the rich cultural and spiritual interests and driving passions of human beings. The effort to answer this question led Jung to formulate his own theory as a counterproposal to Freud's. The term Jung chose to speak about the deployment of psychic energy and its redistribution from one form to another in the course of development was *transformation*. In German the word is *Wandlung*. Hence the title of his book, *Wandlungen und Symbole der Libido*. *Wandlung* means "change," typically change of form. Psychic energy, Jung argued in this early work, can assume many forms, just as energy does in the physical world. It is an expression of the life force—the Will, following Schopenhauer—that animates human bodies and moves them in all the complicated ways humans behave. In itself, libido is not attached to any specific drive or motivation. So the real question becomes how to account for the variety of motivations and behaviors human beings display. For Freud, all could be reduced to sexuality and its sublimation; for Jung it could not. Jung was searching for a mechanism that could transfer and dispense energy from one channel to another. This mechanism, he thought, would be internal to the psyche, part of a growing, balancing, self-adjusting process. The psyche initiates its own transformations, Jung concluded, and these have many aims and purposes, sexual fulfillment being only one of them. Other forms of human activity have their own goals, their own pleasures.

It would take Jung some years to work out the details of his argument, but for our purposes I can pass over them and offer the final conclusion with a brief quotation from *Symbols of Transformation*. Jung inserted this passage when he revised the original text in 1952: "Except when motivated by external necessity, the will to suppress or repress the natural instincts, or rather to overcome their predominance (*superbia*) and lack of coordination (*concupiscentia*), derives from a spiritual source; in other words, the determining factor is the numinous primordial images."[11]

The notion is that the archetypal images transcend the drives and harness or coordinate them (exactly what does not happen in pathological cases). In healthy psyches, these primordial images grip a person's consciousness with the force of instinct, and even the biologically based drives cannot resist or overcome them. They arise within the psyche itself in the form of archetypal projections (such as Mellon's projection onto the figure of Schweitzer) and numinous experiences, which traditionally have been formulated as myths or religious doctrines and rituals. These images, then, have the effect of redirecting psychic energy into new pathways. Each of the patterns of behavior, fantasies, and thoughts that originate with archetypal images has a will and an aim of its own. It is these images, which behave like instincts, that account for the creations of culture, for social structure, and for the content of religious doctrines and values. In other words, Jung saw human nature as fundamentally invested with spiritual energy that is given form by archetypal images.

The etymology of the word *transformation* is instructive. It is made up of two Latin words, *trans* and *forma*. In Latin, *trans* means "across, over, on the other side." I think here of a river. To carry something across the river, one "trans-ports" it. In turn, this Latin word descends from the stem *tra-*, which has cognates in Sanskrit, Celtic, and German. It is a basic word, a primal utterance. A term like this is necessary for consciousness and therefore must be included in every language. The English word "through" is rooted in this stem. In general, then, *trans* communicates the sense of "from one place, person, thing, or state to another,"[12] as in the psychoanalytic term "transference" (meaning "to carry over" a psychic image from one interpersonal context to another). But *trans* also can be stretched to signify "beyond," as in the words "transcendence" and "transpersonal." This locates something as being on the other side of the river, "over there." When people linked this word to *form*—a word descended from the Latin *forma,* meaning "form, figure, shape, image, mold, stamp"—it indicated a change from one figure or image to another. Probably this at first was rather concrete. At one time, the word *forma* meant the shape of a shoe. If one wanted to give shoes a different shape, in order to improve their style or to approach the Platonic ideal of Beauty a little more closely, one's imagination could be employed to bring another shape over from across the river of possibility and apply it to the shoes in the workshop. Then one would have trans-formed them.

This term was found to be extremely useful for thinking about change in many arenas of life. In theater, for instance, transformation refers to a change in character; in zoology, it denotes a change of form in animal life; in mathematics, it means a change of form without alteration in quality or value; in physics, it can refer to a change in form from liquid to gas, for instance, or to a change in energy from one form to another; and, in reference to electricity, it means the change in current due to a transformer. The word has many applications. Small wonder that it was taken up by psychology, too.

Jung was drawn to analogies between psychology and physics. For him, the word *transformation* referred to a change of psychic energy from one form to another, much as physicists use it to describe changes in energy from mechanical to electrical. Common to all particular forms of energy in psychology, as in physics, is the underlying fact of energy itself, which Jung considered, again as in physics, to be subject to the law of conservation. Energy cannot simply disappear from the psychic system. If it is lost to consciousness, it is to be found in the unconscious.

What Jung had uncovered by excavating the pre-Oedipal layers of the psyche—by "tackling the mother"[13]—was a level of psychic object and process that underlay even Freud's famous infantile sexuality. By analyzing psychotic patients at the Burghölzli Klinik and comparing their bizarre mythological images and ritualistic behaviors with anthropological accounts of primitive customs and behavior, he discovered a layer of psyche that is not only pre-sexual but even pre-instinctual. Movements like rhythmic swaying, gesturing, scratching, and sucking are irreducible to any specific instinctual activity—nourishment, sexuality, etc.—but rather are tied into all of them. Musical performance and sexual behavior, for example, have many things in common—rhythm, movements of the body, feelings—but it is not the case that the former is a sublimation of the latter. Rather, both draw on the same reservoir of human behavioral patterns and energies.

This breakthrough to the truly primordial level of the psyche was decisive for Jung and gave him the courage to challenge his revered mentor, Freud. Now he could say that transformation is primary and not secondary (it is not mere sublimation), and eventually that transformation is driven by a force, a will, that has its own goal—namely, the creation of the psychological individual. What we see in the lives of people like William Mellon is how a figure like Albert Schweitzer, a numinous archetypal image of the self, gathers energy to itself like a magnet, transforms it into a new set of ambitions and motivations, and gives life new direction and meaning.

As an interlude, I want to acknowledge that what Jung created in his theory of the psyche was a psychologically based version of Plato's philosophical vision of human nature and the transcendent Forms. In the *Republic*, Plato teaches that there are three types of people among the citizenry of the *polis:* those who are mostly motivated by economic gain and the sensual pleasures that money can buy; those who are intent on gaining power and enjoying fame and celebrity; and those who prefer to observe life at a distance, to reflect on experience, and to pursue wisdom—the philosophers. However, everybody is partly motivated by each of these desires for pleasure, power, and wisdom. The person who does best is the one who manages to keep all three in balance and is able to satisfy each without succumbing to the tyranny of any one of them. This is not easy, because each is powerful and compelling. Sensuality easily can come to dominate life and become one's chief end. (Jung felt this had happened to Freud, at least in his theory of human nature. His mind had been captivated by the divinity of sensuality, by the pleasure principle.) Similarly, power and celebrity can take over and become the prime motivation in all human relationships and dealings. (Adler, the theorist of power, in a sense worshipped this god.) The love of wisdom, too, can become one-sided and can distort life to the point of denying one's normal desires for some sensual pleasure and a bit of power. (Religious fanatics and ideologues, as well as some academic philosophers, fall into this group.) Jung would agree with Plato that the goal is to achieve balance among the instincts, to offer each its due in appropriate measure, and to strive for wholeness rather than perfection.

But what can harness these three powerful drives and temper them? How can wholeness be achieved? For Plato, it was clear that the philosopher should be in charge of the "republic," inner and outer. This is because the philosopher is a person who truly has followed the path indicated by Diotima (through Socrates) in the *Symposium* and has experienced the reality of the Forms. According to Socrates, Diotima taught that the medium by which a person is drawn to the ultimate Form, the Beautiful, is Eros. After being drawn first to many beautiful objects in the sensate world, the reflective person will realize that what is desired above all is not this or that object, which may embody the Form of beauty for a while, but rather Beauty itself. Thus, in being led from concrete object to abstract realization, the philosopher comes to love Beauty itself and even to recognize the identity between Truth and Beauty. For Plato, the vision of Beauty is the transformative experience which allows the philosopher (famously Socrates) to strike a harmonious balance among the desires for pleasure, power, and wisdom. The transformative image of Beauty has the capacity to hold the warring factions together and to elicit unity of aim among them. It transforms disunity and competitive striving, moving them toward harmony and unity of purpose. The transformative image pulls the various disparate energies together and gives them an overall direction.

While Jung's depth psychology is fed by sources other than Plato and philosophical reflection—most importantly, by clinical experiences and observation—it has many points of intellectual contact with Plato. Not the least of these is a common appreciation for the transforming power of that which Jung would call archetypal images and Plato the Forms. Where Jung and Plato part company I shall indicate later.

A transformative image, then, is an image that has the capacity to redirect the flow of psychic energy and to change its specific form of manifestation. The way in which this image relates to the instinctual needs of the individual is critical, for this will determine whether the constellation supports balance and wholeness or represses aspects of human nature and results in one-sidedness and distortion. This brings us to the question of the role of culture and society, and especially religion, in the psychological life of the individual. All but isolated individuals live in large and small collective groups and organizations. These provide opportunities for accessing transformative images, but they also create hazards for individuals who are striving to live their wholeness.

Cultures and religions are repositories of transformative images from the past. This is evident to all sensitive students of human culture and history. From time immemorial, the cultures of humankind have housed and treasured the primordial images of the collective unconscious and made them available to people in their religious mysteries, sacred rites, and rituals. When a person experiences one of these images deeply, it has a profound effect upon consciousness. F. M. Cornford, the preeminent interpreter of Greek philosophy and especially of Plato, summarizes Plato's doctrine of transformation as follows:

> The final object—beyond physical, moral, and intellectual beauty—is the Beautiful itself. This is revealed to intuition "suddenly." The language here recalls the culminating revelation of the Eleusinian mysteries—the disclosure of sacred symbols or figures as the divinities in a sudden blaze of light. This object is eternal, exempt from change and relativity, no longer

manifested in anything else, in any living thing, or in earth or heaven, but always "by itself," entirely unaffected by the becoming or perishing of anything that may partake of its character. The act of acquaintance with it is the vision of a spectacle, whereby the soul has contact with the ultimate object of Eros and enters into possession of it. So man becomes immortal in the divine sense. As in the *Republic,* the union of the soul with Beauty is called a marriage—the sacred marriage of the Eleusinia—of which the offspring are, not phantoms like those images of goodness that first inspired love of the beautiful person, but true virtue, the virtue which is wisdom. For Plato believed that the goal of philosophy was that man should become a god, knowing good from evil with such clearness and certainty as could not fail to determine the will infallibly.[14]

In this inspiring passage, Cornford compares the individual path of the philosopher to the collective path of the ancient Greek mystery religion at Eleusis, which was dedicated to the Mother Goddess, Demeter. In the mysteries, we can recognize the central role played by religion in constellating the transformative archetypal image for many individuals. A person is prepared ritually for exposure to the sacred symbols and images; if this preparation is propitious, a vision ensues that is the occasion for a "marriage" between the soul and the object of its deepest longing. From this union transformation results. It is the same, Cornford writes, for the individual philosopher who contemplates the Beautiful. The soul and the object of contemplation become united, and the soul is transformed.

Because religions possess and employ such powerful images of transformation in their rituals, they can channel psychic energy on a massive collective level. They also collect a surplus of archetypal energy from the projections of their adherents, and this typically is used to build up and enrich the institutional organization and the clerics in it. This surplus of energy can be used well, for good works, for healing, for initiation and transformation; or poorly, for selfish, sexual, or power motives, being directed toward misguided ends. Cult leaders of recent fame—Jim Jones, David Koresch, and Marshall Applewhite—are cases in point of the latter possibility. Jerry Garcia of the Grateful Dead is a mixed case.

As Plato and Jung knew only too well, cultures and organizations can distort human nature as well as help to fulfill it. One has only to think of foot binding in Old China or segregation in the Old South. Corporate America has performed similar distortions on individuals in our own time. But what is the criterion for deciding whether the transformative images of traditional cultures and religions, ancient or modern, foster health or illness? On what basis shall we be prepared to deny genital mutilation to the vituperative yet committed women of Central Africa who insist on this practice for custom's sake? For both Jung and Plato, the test would be pragmatic: do the transformative images that are being held up and promoted by a specific culture support or thwart the individual psyche's urge toward wholeness? Do they coordinate and balance the various "faculties" (Plato) or "instinct groups" (Jung) and direct them in a manner that allows for optimal fulfillment, under the aegis of an overarching statement of meaning and purpose, in the styles of living they help to shape? Plato witnessed directly the intolerance of advocates of traditional religion toward an innovative statement of the ideal in the trial and death of his hero, Socrates. Jung analyzed the central transformative images of his own religious tradition, Christianity, and, like Socrates with Greek religion and myth, found the images lacking something essential.

While Jung recognized the image of Christ as a transformative archetypal image of great power and persuasiveness, he also judged it to be incomplete because it did not sufficiently symbolize wholeness. It lacked *shadow*, in his judgment. Jung's argument, made over and over in his later writings, is that the Christian God image, the Trinity, betrays an absence of shadow integration. It is wholly "good," and evil is defined as mere *privatio boni*, the absence of good. For Jung, as for Plato, a transformative image that represses, neglects, or denies important features of human nature will not do the job of integrating the whole person and balancing all the aspects and forces of the personality. Clitoridectomy denies normal sexual satisfaction to women, even if culturally it signifies rank and proper initiation into adult womanhood. It denies more than it gives. The large modern corporation demands that individual executives and workers, to qualify for higher wages and job advancement, sacrifice all to the workplace— uprooting families, working eighty-hour weeks, traveling interminably. This system gives back a lot of rewards to some but also denies basic values inherent in wholeness and a life of meaning. In all three cases, there is an absence of shadow awareness.

To be fair, one must admit that Jung was right about the dogmatic Christ image, the image of a perfect man in whom there was no sin; but he was off the mark with respect to the image of Jesus in the Gospels. In the Synoptic Gospels (Matthew, Mark, and Luke), Jesus is depicted as the Son of Man, as a person who mingles with common people, who eats and drinks freely with publicans and prostitutes, whose first miracle is to turn water into wine for the added merriment of a wedding party, who breaks the rigid religious rules regarding the Sabbath, and who can display anger to the point of being intemperate. He also treats the body, healing the physically sick, the blind, the diseased. In short, he is shown to be fully embodied, living a human life and suffering the common human experience of death. He breathes, he sweats, he laughs and cries. This is not an image of abstract and inhuman perfection. If anything, the Gospel writers went out of their way to create an image of a flesh-and-blood individual. Jesus is a man of action, engaged with issues of his day, involved in the human condition at all levels. With regard to the portrait of Jesus in the three Synoptic Gospels, Jung plainly errs in his judgment that it lacks shadow.

Where Jung does correctly identify a problem is in the dogmatic version of Christ, as this image was elaborated in New Testament times by Paul and his early followers and by later church authorities, theologians, and Councils. The focus shifted away from the human Jesus of Nazareth to theological problems such as redemption from sin and atonement (Christ had to be the perfect sacrifice, otherwise God's justice would not have been satisfied). The puzzles concerning Christ's two natures, one human and one divine, and his relations within the Godhead (a Trinity) gave rise to a host of careful philosophical and theological distinctions but obscured the Jesus image of the Synoptic Gospels. Moreover, the early church's insistence on creating a biblical canon that would include so many disparate writings—the Pentateuch, words of the prophets, and the Psalms, along with the Synoptic Gospels, the Fourth Gospel, the writings of Paul, other epistles, and even the bizarre Book of Revelation—ended by placing Jesus in a Procrustean context. The transformative image of Jesus of Nazareth was compromised by its setting. Jesus had to become the answer to Old Testament prophesies, the fulfillment of ancient Messianic promises, and the Son of God rather than the Son of Man. All of this had the effect of at once elevating the image and eviscerating it, draining away its uniqueness and pumping it up with theological and philosophical notions. The human Jesus got lost in the interpretation, and the quest for the historical Jesus so far has been unsuccessful in recovering him.

Nevertheless, what was made available by the Christian tradition as it grew and eventually became dominant in the Roman Empire was an image of transformative power that profoundly altered the West's values and basic assumptions about life. It is beyond dispute that Christianity transformed classical culture. In doing so, it redefined the terms of good and evil, drew a shroud over the body, and clothed the naked pagan statue. Christianity offered an account of history based upon the fall of man and the consequences of original sin. It also offered hope for salvation and a promise of eternal life beyond the grave. It transformed the vision of the nature and destiny of humankind, and it defined the means of grace. Nothing in Western culture was left untouched. But the transformative image at the center of Christianity—Jesus of Nazareth—shifted to the periphery in the march toward social and cultural hegemony. By the time the famous image of the Renaissance Pope Leo X, who in all his magisterial earthy sensuality and secular splendor and power was painted brilliantly by Raphael, one must wonder whether this figure has anything in common, let alone shares a spiritual perspective, with Jesus of Nazareth. The transformative image itself has been transformed, and the time grows ripe for reformation.

Both the Reformation and the Renaissance, more or less coinciding historically, were efforts to reach back to origins. The Reformation of Christianity attempted to recapture the spirit of the early church—its purity of purpose and its simplicity. On the left wing of the Reformation were, in fact, communistic movements that recalled the scene in the Book of Acts in which all believers placed their worldly possessions into a common account. The Renaissance, on the other hand, looked back to the ancient Greeks for inspiration and sought to recapture the fullness of the human form, with its beauty and sensuality. While both sides were blessed with genius aplenty and an outpouring of inspiration and energy, their joint existence signaled a major crisis in Western culture. A dead end had been reached, as beautiful in some ways as the Middle Ages had been; to go forward, Western culture was forced to reach far back into the past for transformative images. What the Renaissance discovered, or uncovered again, was Plato's ideal of the Beautiful, *tò Agathón;* what the Reformation recovered was the Bible. Each became a transformative image for one of these movements.

What the transformative image offers is a pattern for arranging psychic energy along specific lines. For the Reformation, the Bible served this purpose. New translations in local languages proliferated, and preaching from the Bible and rigorous Bible study became the guides by which life in Protestant communities was shaped. A new interpretation of the biblical text often would result in a new denomination, yet common to all sects was the transformative image itself, the Bible. As long as one could locate a viewpoint or a doctrine in the sacred text, one was on firm ground. This would establish and justify a lifestyle, a set of rules and laws of conduct, a behavioral norm. Some of these were relatively generous and life-enhancing, but many were repressive, life-denying, and punitive. The Counter Reformation followed suit, also moving toward intolerance and rigidity. Human nature chafed under these burdens. In seeking relief, people created the famous subterfuges of eighteenth- and nineteenth-century European culture. It was into this world that Freud and Jung were born, and both were famously unaccepting of hypocrisy.

Jung's critique of the Christ image—that it lacks shadow—derives from his personal experience in the Swiss Reformed Church. His opinion of this religious denomination, in which he grew up and in which his father and six of his uncles and one grandfather were pastors, was that it was without life. The mainsprings of psychic energy no longer were organized by or contained within it. It did not move the emotions or touch the heart. It was a dead letter, a mere convention. What this church, and Swiss culture generally, supported was Respectability—a new god of the age, Jung called it—but Christianity had little commanding influence on individuals or on society as a whole. Who wanted to hear the words of Jesus, or pick up a cross and follow him? Nor did the church's image of Jesus become an important figure in Jung's inner life, which was much more occupied with Gnostic and alchemical images and persons. From a certain analytical distance, he could appreciate and even find resonance with some standard Christian doctrines, such as the Trinity, and some rituals, such as the Mass; but, so far as is known, these did not touch his inner life in a transformative way. For Jung, the church's image of Jesus, or Christ, had an unreal quality; it was too abstract, too light, perfect, and translucent to move him. The religious tradition of his family and his culture no longer could persuade him or contain his psychic energy. He was a modern man, and he spoke as one who was in search of his soul. Yet, as we saw in Jung's transforming second active imagination, the image of Jesus crucified played a key role in his midlife metamorphosis.

It was Jung's estimate that religious traditions generally were losing their power to convince and to provide transformative images. While many people continue to adhere to them, many do so simply out of habit and for the sake of respectability. It is like going to the opera—one goes in order to be seen. Others, of course, are genuinely contained by, and find resources in, the images provided. But in modern industrialized and technological societies, these are ever fewer in number. The loss of religious life is a central problem of modernity. Where, then, can one look for symbols of transformation? Ours is a time not, in this sense, unlike that of Socrates. The old religion has become a formality, so where does one turn for the transformative image needed to harmonize the disparate parts of the psyche and impart a sense of direction and meaning? Jung gave up on organized religion and looked to private inner spiritual experience.

The "way of the dream" is one approach to the problem of discovering effective transformative images for the modern individual. To those not schooled in this way, it will seem improbable that dream images could function as transformative images in the same way that traditional religious symbols do. Dreams are ephemeral, constantly changing, a symptom of the flux of psychic process rather than stable forms that can organize conscious attitudes and behavior. And yet, to the careful student of dreams, it is apparent that occasionally a symbolic dream occurs that stands out from the rest. Jung was wise to distinguish between little dreams and big dreams. A big dream is one that has the potential to become a transformative image.

A transformative image, I remind the reader, is one that channels psychic energy and will into specific attitudes, activities, and goals. In order to have this potential, an image must have roots deep and broad in the psyche as a whole. A transforming dream image is an archetypal image that manages to capture the element of wholeness in an individual's life and give it specific shape and direction.

Jung himself was gifted with many big dreams, which guided his inner development in essential ways, but he is not alone. Many people who pay close attention to their dreams for an extended period of time—years, decades—find that they have big dreams, and it is not an uncommon happening in analysis. For example, I had a dream while I was in training analysis that has never left me. I have used it as a meditation many times since then. In the dream,

I am in a large assembly hall. The room is packed, and the audience is waiting for the speaker to appear on stage. At the appointed time, a gentleman who looks like the late sage Krishnamurti walks to the center. He is holding a canvas about six feet wide and three feet high with a simple drawing on it. The drawing is a single unbroken line that depicts a house, a rock, and a tree. The distinguished speaker asks the audience to volunteer interpretations of this picture. A few people do so but without much success, and so the lecturer himself says: "You can see that the drawing depicts several objects, but it is made with one unbroken line. This means that all things are connected." Pause. "And what connects them is— love."

The dream ended with this lesson. It is a teaching that is not especially novel or surprising, given the speaker, and if this incident had occurred in waking life I might have forgotten it soon enough. But because it came to me in a dream—specifically to me alone—it made a strong impression.

The dream needs no specialized psychological interpretation. It speaks for itself. If one penetrates into its message, it can be transformative. A whole world view is embedded in this dream. It is an image that expresses the universal connections beneath the multiplicity of the phenomenal world of appearances. In the numinal world, everything is linked by love, even if, in appearance, objects and people are seen as separate and distinct. Both levels are true. A house is not a tree is not a stone. You are not me, I am not my brother, he is not his neighbor. . . . This is true enough. Distinctions are important, even essential, for consciousness. Good fences make good neighbors. And yet, this teaching holds that, at a less obvious level, we are all made of the same stuff—same atoms, same molecules, same energy systems—and that the whole is held together by a glue that in this dream is called "love." Obviously what is meant is not romantic love, erotic energy, or sexual libido, even if romantic love and sexual libido also draw us together and often lead to a feeling of oneness and a recognition of the unity of all things. But sexual libido is only one kind of love energy. It is the general energy of love— libido itself—that is the bond, the glue of the universe of objects, inanimate and animate. Sexual love is one instance of love, kinship libido another, *agape* yet another. The dream teaches that love is not only a personal emotion; it is an impersonal bond, an emotional force that works throughout the cosmos toward unity and staying connected.

I share this dream as an example of a potentially transformative image. It implies a vision of life and has practical implications. In another dream about the same time, I was given the chance to witness the original creation of matter. At the bottom of a deep hole in the ground, two elements—gases—were brought into play with one another, and they created what in the dream was called "original matter." This was a scientific experiment. Again, the notion of union is expressed in this dream image. I puzzled about these dreams for years, remembering always that Heraclitus said that war is the mother of all things. How to square conflict with unifying energy, hate with love? It is an ancient problem. Some philosophers, like Empedocles, wanted to say that both are necessary. One force unites and draws things together; the other separates and differentiates them. My own conclusion, following Jung's suggestions and my dreams, is that there are two levels. At the level of consciousness, differentiation is a crucial value; but at the level of the deeper psyche, within the self, love and unity predominate. We actually live in two worlds simultaneously.

Dreams offer potentially transformative images to consciousness, but the outcome depends upon the work a person does with them. One reason religious images have such a profound effect on individuals and on whole collectives is that they are repeated endlessly (Freud, misunderstanding the purpose of religious ritual, said compulsively). The sheer repetition of the Mass, day after day, Sunday after Sunday, year after year, in exactly the same form creates patterns in the conscious and unconscious psychic energy systems that become indelible. Compared to this organized round of rite and ritual, the single, once-only, unique experience of a dream image appears to be highly evanescent. But if the dream image is taken up by consciousness, retained, worked on (not necessarily compulsively, but regularly) over a period of time, it has the potential to transform conscious attitudes and, following that, behavior and motivation. The psyche has the capacity to regulate itself and to provoke its own development. This is where Jung parted company with Freud.

It is my argument, throughout this book, that a person's destiny—which is made from the qualities and markings that end up establishing themselves as the deepest etchings of character, mission, and meaning in life, the features that define a particular life as unique—

is importantly, perhaps most essentially, constituted by a series of transformative images and experiences. What happens is that a person's integrity and potential as a unique human being become realized through these transformations. One becomes the person one most essentially and uniquely is, by means of the images that draw one's psychic energy into a certain configuration of attitude, behavior, and motivation.

If these integrating transformative images for some reason disintegrate—through disillusionment, trauma, devastating contradictions, violations of whatever sort—the personality falls to pieces. A process of disintegration sets in, and the various part-personalities and instinctual drives take over. They become warring members in a house divided. This is the tragedy of psychological disintegration. It may happen early or late in life. The only remedy is to start over again from the base of the personality's structure and rebuild from the ground up, using new images that can contain the parts of the person and move them ahead in life. A modern example of this on a huge collective level is Germany in the aftermath of World War II. Its self-image as a high culture of civilized conduct and moral values was utterly destroyed, as its national and cultural integrity dissolved in the mayhem of Nazi evil and psychopathic madness. To reconstitute itself as a civil state, it needed first to admit its guilt, then to accept the punishment of universal condemnation and to atone for the past. Only from this ground-zero position could the country hope to begin rebuilding the bases of its culture. The Germans today are still in the earliest stages of this development.

What happened in Germany and Europe in the 1930s and 1940s has universal human implications. When the spiritual history of our times is written, the Holocaust will go down as the major "religious event" of the twentieth century. In the long stretch of Western history, it will be seen as a defining moment, one as decisive as the Crucifixion—a historical event that becomes a symbol of transformation. Since the Holocaust, we have not been able to think truly about the spiritual condition of the West—indeed, of humankind generally—without considering its awesome message. It is an event whose very darkness illuminates the radical and evil one-sidedness of conscious development of human beings to this point. The Holocaust's critical mass of intense suffering places upon each of us an implacable obligation for deep change, for transformation of consciousness. Each individual must wake up to the need to surrender the ego and the nation to a broader sense of the human family and of the ecosystem in which we all must live together. For human cultures to transform, each individual must grapple with the inner forces of good and evil and must confront the demon of ego-centricity, whether this is defined by one's own immediate physical existence or by tribal group or national interests. The Holocaust is a cry that calls us to a new stage of *global* human development.

Much in how individual lives turn out depends upon how transformative images—whether abstract like the Holy Sacrifice, a figure like Aion, or a human being like Albert Schweitzer—are received and developed. The images embody complexity and the potential for further development.

The notion that archetypal images themselves also need development and conscious intervention would haunt Jung for the rest of his life. In what was a late, extended active imagination, recorded for publication as *Answer to Job,* he wrestled with the God image of the biblical traditions, with Yahweh himself. According to Jung's view, Yahweh was blind to his anima and had an inferior feeling function, just as Jung did. Like Jung, too, Yahweh put himself through death by crucifixion in order to redeem his Eros and his emotional connection to humankind. Finally, as in Jung's psyche, the blind anima of biblical tradition, having regained her place in the patriarchal pantheon of Father, Son, and Holy Spirit as the deified and elevated Virgin Mother, is transforming consciousness in our time. Jung must have felt he was assisting this development in collective consciousness by suffering through the experience of writing this text, which came to him in a burst of inspiration during a brief period of time while he was recovering from his second heart attack in his mid-seventies. He was recapitulating his own inner development and trying to use it to heal his ailing religious tradition and to move it forward into a new stage of development around the transformative image of quaternity.[15] For Jung, his personal transformation and the collective transformation of Christianity became intertwined.

The key point is that, while transformative images mold and shape our attitudes, values, horizons of meaning, and purposes, and in some cases even provide us with the experience of deification, they also are in need of, and subject to, transformation. Immemorial and timeless they may be, but as they are drawn into encounters with us and we with them, they too will change. Here Jung parts company with Plato and comes close to modern process philosophers and theologians. The alchemy of this interaction produces what we call individuation, a process of mutual evolution toward wholeness.

CHAPTER 3

Transformative Relationships

> *Wholeness is a combination of I and You, and these*
> *show themselves to be parts of a transcendent unity*
> *whose nature can only be grasped symbolically.*
>
> —C. G. Jung

She is dreaming.

A doorbell rings, and she walks through the house to answer it. Friends have arrived for a visit. She greets them enthusiastically and leads them to the guest rooms in the basement, which until then she had not realized existed. The basement is a discovery. It is much larger than the house itself—six times as big!—and beautifully laid out with wide corridors and elegant guest suites. (In actuality, her house has no such basement.) As she escorts her friends into this space, she warns them of the water at the entrance. Boots are required to pass over the threshold.

"Where shall we stay?" her friend inquires.

"I would recommend the suite on the far end, to the left. It has such beautiful views of the ocean and the terraced gardens. On the other side, of course, you can see the mountains, but I think this view is nicer." Odd, it seems to her, the "basement" is above ground. As they enter, they find many friends and colleagues of her husband's wandering through the halls, seeming to be busy with various matters. Her husband has been build-ing this space for some time and is moving forward toward the front of the house as he proceeds. His work is nearly complete. He greets their friends, hammer and saw in hand, and helps them with their luggage.

The dream ends here, and the next day she marvels at the large space beneath their home.

The woman's husband had been busy with some projects that he had not had time to tell her about in the few days before the dream. In their mutual unconscious—the large basement under their home—this was noted. The views from the basement, surprisingly, look out on a world that the house above ground in actuality does not share. The psyche is an open space, and the farther inward you go, the more you find yourself outside.

Relationships have many levels and aspects, and not all of them are easily accessible to consciousness. When a relationship begins, one may worry about the role of projection and "transference"— that is, effects carried over from past relationships. Also, images of an ideal are created by the psyche, using the hair, eyes, and other personal qualities of a person one has just met. After forming a rela-tionship and living in it for a time, one expects less projection, less idealization, and resolution of transference or its flight to another person. But, even then, there are levels of unconsciousness, and elu-sive interactions continue. People, it turns out, are connected in many surprising and enduring ways, and they continue to discover new facets endlessly.

Before embarking on what is for me the difficult task of exploring the transformative effects of personal relationships—difficult be-cause so much material lies in the territory of intimacy, which must remain unspoken and shrouded in confidentiality and in personal and even professional discretion—let me restate my general view-point. Psychological trans-formation is the "passing over" (Latin, *trans*) of psychic energy from one "organized pattern" (Latin, *forma*) to another. Although this can happen at many times in life, my focus is on psychological transformation in adulthood. In the first two chapters, I argued that the means by which this is accomplished is the transforming image. Images arise from the archetypal collective unconscious—whether "inner" or "outer" is immaterial—like activated imaginal disks in the pupa of a butterfly, and these create the bridge between the old psychological constellation and a new one. The transformation can be conceptualized as a passage from a "false self" to a "true self." The formation of the mature adult self imago installs a new sense of selfhood. A new vocation may be born from this, or an earlier one may be confirmed at a deeper and more convincing level. The former path we see in the life of William Mellon, who experienced the transforming image of Albert Schweitzer and became a medical missionary in Haiti. The latter option is evident in the biography of Carl Jung, who experienced the image of Aion and at midlife became a new kind of teacher and healer; and in the story of Rainer Maria Rilke, who heard a voice in the wind speaking about angelic orders and became a modern Orpheus. Jung speaks of this transformation as a contemporary instance of an ancient spiritual mystery ("deification") because the transformative images transcend the ego. Through this process of transformation, people assume their destined specific imagos, which will shape their adult lives. The transformation process extends over a long period of time but typically begins with a powerful symbolic experience that is triggered by physical and psychological factors which become active during adulthood and behave like change hormones. One of the most powerful of these factors is the experience of intimate relationship.

The full adult imago that emerges is a pattern of attitudes, self-assessments, and motivations; it consists of aspects of the psyche that previously have lain partially or completely dormant and undeveloped (not repressed[1]) in the unconscious. The post-adolescent phase of development can be looked upon as another type of latency period,[2] much like the one that Freud and Jung saw as typical of children before they reach puberty. The imago that develops out of the transformative process will draw forth, contain, and channel libido into what potentially is a person's realized wholeness. It is typical of this transformational era that it begins dramatically, with an announcement of endings and glimpses of things to come, then passes through an extended period of liminality, and concludes with the rapid configuration and emergence of the newly formed imago. In Rilke's case, as I showed in the first chapter, the imago emerged dramatically after ten years of pupation, when, in the early months of 1922, the *Duino Elegies* and *The Sonnets to Orpheus* suddenly were completed.

My account of psychological transformation in adulthood so far mostly has ignored the important factor of *context*. What is the context in which the transforming person lives? I said in the introduction that other factors must be taken into account besides the seemingly spontaneous and autonomous happenings—dreams, intuitions, visions, possessions—within the individual psyche. Biologists have ascertained that, in the timing of the termination of diapause in the pupa of the butterfly, environmental factors such as light, warmth, and the amount of moisture available play key roles in triggering the hormones that set off the final burst of imago formation. So it is, too, with psychological transformation. In the period before and during the early stages of adolescence, for example, social and familial factors play an important role in triggering and shaping the adolescent experience. Factors such as social expectation and lifestyle, economic situation, physical and medical conditions, political events like warfare, and personal relationships play a large role in the timing and outcome of the adult transformation process. Beyond that, these factors constitute the matrix within which the transforming images arise and the context in which the transformation process takes place.

This chapter focuses specifically on personal relationships in adulthood as the context of transformation. The power of Eros to constellate the psyche and to change human lives has been acknowledged from time immemorial. Intimate relationships are perhaps the richest environments for psychological transformation throughout human life, including adulthood. While this is a difficult and sensitive issue to discuss in a book like this, it must be considered central. It was what Freud touched upon in his theory of sexuality but did not pursue to the fullest extent, because of his aversion to the deeper mysteries of love and his suspicion of transformation. For him sexuality was mostly a biological matter of drive excitation and discharge, not a spiritual one of union and transformation. This latter approach is one that analytical psychology has, in its own mythopoetic as well as psychodynamic way, studied and reflected upon with great interest.

Transference and countertransference in analysis form the context in which analytical psychology has examined transformation most closely. To approach this subject, therefore, I shall turn to a consideration of the practice of psychotherapy, in which the interpersonal relationship between therapist and patient generally is recognized as being the critical factor in therapeutic change. Consideration of the therapy context supplies an occasion for reflecting, albeit somewhat indirectly and discretely, upon the psychological and transformational issues involved in intimate relationships between adults.

Whenever I have asked professional psychotherapists, "What heals in therapy?" the most frequent answer has been "the relationship." The personal relationship between therapist and patient typically is seen as the essential factor upon which change and psychological growth depend. It is as if this is what releases the hormones that stimulate transformation in therapy.

While this seems to be the consensus today, it was not always so. In the early days of psychoanalysis, it was supposed that the analyst's insightful interpretations, which uncovered unconscious thoughts and memories and made them conscious again, played the critical role in producing a cure. Transference was regarded as essential, but not because it offered a "corrective emotional experience," as was later held, but rather because it offered the opportunity for repeating the past and thereby raising the repressed oedipal conflicts to the surface of consciousness and allowing them to be interpreted. Interpretation was the way to make the unconscious conscious and to follow Freud's dictum: "Where the id is, there let the ego be." More light in the dark would release people from their neurotic conflicts. Enlightenment and ego mastery over psychic life were the aims of early Freudian analysis.

Jung too followed this program in his Freudian years. His relationship with Freud got off on the right foot when he passed Freud's test question in their first meeting in 1907. Freud asked him what he thought was the most important factor in psychoanalysis, and he responded without hesitation, "the transference." Freud assured him that he had grasped the main point. The focus of analytic treatment was to be on the fantasy relationship the patient spun around the quiet reflective presence of the doctor. All the love and hate the patient had experienced in childhood with parents—especially with the parent of the other sex—would be repeated in the analytic relationship, suffered all over again, and regurgitated as wish-fulfilling dreams, slips of the tongue, emotional resistance, incestuous longings and memories, and acting-out behaviors. This material would be gathered by the attentive analyst, assembled into a pattern for interpretation, and offered as an explanation for why the patient was suffering from such specific symptoms as hysterical blindness, compulsive acts, obsessive thoughts, etc. The cure was measured by increased rationality, greater ego control, and better insight into chronic behavioral and emotional patterns.

Jung tried to be a good Freudian during their years of collaboration, and he practiced this sort of transference analysis on his less pathological patients. With chronically psychotic patients in the Burghölzli Klinik, however, it proved not useful to interpret transference, and Jung became convinced early on that schizophrenia was an organically based mental disorder that would not yield to transference analysis. Nonetheless, in his private practice and with his healthier and more intellectually gifted patients, he performed what then was considered correct psychoanalysis. But it also quickly became apparent to him that there was more to the relationship in therapy than a one-sided transference. Two psyches are involved in the therapeutic encounter; both are subject to emotional reactions, and both are given to projecting unconscious contents into the other. A new term had to be invented to cover the doctor's involvement in the relationship. Between them, Freud and Jung came up with the somewhat unfortunate and infelicitous term *countertransference* (in German it sounds even worse than in English: *Gegenübertragung*). Over time this would become a doctor's way of saying, "She made me do it!" The clinician's emotional response was seen as a reaction to the patient's original, interfering transference. Eve offered the apple; Adam only responded to the invitation. The doctor does not initiate or even contribute much, according to some versions of this theory.

It now is widely known that Jung was caught up in a troublesome countertransference at the time he met Freud.[3] He was treating a (to him) fascinating young Russian Jewish woman named Sabina Spielrein. She had been sent as an adolescent by her parents to the world-famous Burghölzli Klinik in Zurich and there became a patient of Jung, who was chief psychiatric resident at the time. Spielrein, though not named, appears as an item of concern early in Jung's correspondence with Freud. On October 23, 1906, he wrote, "I am currently treating an hysteric with your method. Difficult case, a 20-year-old Russian girl student, ill for 6 years."[4] Freud showed interest in the symptoms and replied with a detailed analysis of them on October 27. About a year later, Jung again wrote to Freud about a problem he was having with an obsessional patient who had made him the object of her sexual fantasies (October 10, 1907): "Should I continue the treatment, which on her own admission gives her voluptuous pleasure, or should I discharge her?"[5] It is supposed that this is another reference to Spielrein. Freud's letter in response is lost, but Jung's reply indicates that Freud gave him advice which he took to good effect (October 28). One can only imagine that Freud had empathized with Jung's dilemma and counseled making an interpretation and maintaining a neutral analytic attitude.

What Freud and his followers eventually developed as the ideal treatment model was what the American psychoanalyst Merton Gill has called the "one person situation."[6] I call it the "only one psyche in the room" therapy model. The patient's psyche enters the analytic space and occupies it fully by generating free associations, offering dream reports for analysis, presenting resistances, and acting out. The analyst, on the other side, maintains emotional calm and neutrality ("evenly hovering attention") and offers occasional summarizing interpretations. Anything else contributed by the analyst in the way of interpersonal interaction—whether verbal, enacted, or even simply silently felt—is regarded as "contamination" of this ideal analytic space and should be viewed as countertransference reaction and analyzed away.

In Jung's work with the patient Spielrein, there clearly was a lot of contamination. In fact, according to the correspondence published and discussed by Carotenuto,[7] eventually they wandered into a quasi-erotic (no one knows for sure how far they went) relationship. But this occurred after years of psychiatric treatment. It is evident that, during this time, Spielrein had changed from a severely disturbed, mentally ill adolescent patient at the beginning of Jung's treatment into a highly gifted, competent medical doctor and nascent psycho-analyst at the conclusion of their time together in Zurich. Their rela-tionship passed through many phases in the course of the ten years or so they worked together (and even thereafter), evolving from a simple psychiatric patient-doctor relationship to a romanticized younger woman–older man constellation, and then to a mentorship configuration in which Jung was Spielrein's dissertation advisor and helped her to publish her first professional paper. Eventually the rela-tionship evolved into a more distant but always mutually respectful collegial one after Spielrein left Zurich and joined Freud's circle in Vienna. It was this kind of therapeutic relationship—so unorthodox in Freudian terms, so difficult to manage in a professional context, so challenging to the doctor—that stimulated Jung to reform-ulate completely his thinking about the nature and transformative potential of the analytic process. Eventually he came to regard trans-formation in analysis as dependent upon psychic interaction rather than upon detached interpretation. Something must happen in a person's affective psychological experiencing, and not only in her or his thinking, in order to produce transformation.

By 1929, when Jung wrote the article "Problems of Modern Psy-chotherapy" for the Swiss journal *Schweizerisches Medizinisches Jahr-buch,* he had behind him over twenty-five years of clinical experience with the almost infinite variety of cases and interpersonal constella-tions that are offered over the course of a long career in this field. When he wrote this short piece, he was at the peak of his public career as a world-renowned psychiatrist and analytical psychologist. In it, he offered a summary of his experiences as an analyst and as supervisor and teacher of generations of younger analysts. (The range of a senior analyst's experience is greatly extended through his role as a supervisor of younger colleagues' work, and Jung had many students over the long course of his psychiatric career.) In this article, Jung describes four "stages of analysis"—perhaps "dimensions" or "levels" would have been a better term, since these do not necessarily follow one another sequentially—in long-term psychotherapy: confession, elucidation, education, and transformation. Let us consider the first three briefly before moving on to the stage most important for our purposes, transformation.

In Jung's mind, psychotherapy is linked to a religious practice traditionally found in the Roman Catholic church: "The first beginnings of all analytical treatment of the soul are to be found in its prototype, the confessional."[8] Suggested by the term *confession*, too, is the confidential nature of the psychotherapeutic interaction and communication and the opportunity in therapy to speak openly about otherwise carefully guarded secrets, both acts and thoughts. To one degree or another, all schools of psychotherapy have this stage in common, although behavioral and cognitive modes tend to downplay it.

Elucidation, rather than *interpretation*, is the term Jung preferred to use for the second stage, perhaps because of *interpretation's* strong Freudian connotation. By *elucidation* he means understanding and explaining the patient's transference á la Freud, as a "carry-over" (trans-ference) from past to present, from parent to analyst. In this stage of treatment, the analyst explains the present psychological situation of the patient reductively—that is, by referring to formative persons and scenes from childhood. Elucidation becomes necessary in therapy when, after a person confesses, transference begins to emerge. The analyst is experienced as an intimate confidante with moral and psychological authority. The early analysts discovered rather quickly that catharsis arising from confession was not enough to produce permanent healing. It might alleviate symptoms temporarily, but it did not altogether cure the patient. In order to go on in analysis, the transference had to be lifted up into consciousness and analyzed. "The patient falls into a sort of childish dependence from which he cannot defend himself even by rational insight . . . Obviously we are dealing with a neurotic formation, a new symptom directly induced by the treatment."[9] This bond with the analyst is based upon unconscious incest fantasies, and it is to Freud's everlasting credit, Jung acknowledged, that he uncovered this fact of psychological life. Jung himself had experienced this with Freud, a father figure.[10] Elucidation serves to return the authority vested in the analyst back to the patient's ego, thereby strengthening it and making it more autonomous. This stage of analysis helps a person grow out of childhood and assume the power and responsibility of adulthood. It also uncovers and brings into full consciousness the shadow side of the psyche: "It is the most effective antidote imaginable to all the idealistic illusions about the nature of man."[11] Elucidation of transference has a corrosive effect upon an unrealistic and inflated conscious attitude and grounds it in reality. It is a powerful tool for change, and Jung continued to believe in using it vigorously in the treatment of neurotic (and especially, of young) patients.

When the stage of elucidation has been traversed, the patient is left with the task of making a new adaptation to life. The old habits of idealization and childish wishful thinking have been unmasked and dismantled, and now a new approach to the tasks of living is required. Analysis enters a third stage at this point, *education*. Education is the Adlerian stage, Jung says, and it is an almost inevitable consequence of elucidation. Elucidation, the Freudian stage, frees energies that were tied up in neurotic childishness and dependency on external authorities; and the question now becomes where to invest this free energy, what to do with it. Adler recognized the need for social education beyond the understanding of the unconscious and insight into its primitive workings. He was fundamentally an educator who sought to help his patients make a better adaptation in their everyday lives through, first, achieving high self-esteem and, second, investing it in broad social interest. Here the analyst becomes an educator and helps to shape behavior and adaptation to social ideals and realities.

Transformation, Jung's meaningful and creative contribution, is the fourth stage of analysis. In it, the therapist is prepared to lead the patient one step further, beyond the issues of ego-building and adaptation to the collective and social dimensions of life. This stage is not suitable for everyone, and generally it is reserved for patients in the second half of life who already have made an adequate adaptation and contribution to society and who are not pathologically impaired. It focuses on individuation and on releasing the person's unique personality from its bondage to conscious and unconscious restrictions. Here Jung brings out his views on the dialectical interaction that takes place between analyst and analysand: "In any effective psychological treatment the doctor is bound to influence the patient; but this influence can only take place if the patient has a reciprocal influence on the doctor. You can exert no influence if you are not susceptible to influence. It is futile for the doctor to shield himself from the influence of the patient."[12] Transformation is a two-way process, Jung explains. Both the doctor and the patient are affected by the profound engagement that takes place between them when this stage of treatment is entered.

There are challenges in this stage beyond the ones usual in psychotherapy. Sometimes a power question arises in this relationship, and it becomes a contest of whose personality will prevail. Occasionally, Jung hints darkly, the patient's psyche assimilates the doctor's, and more than one therapist's professional and personal life has been ruined by falling victim to the psychological impact of a patient's unconscious. It is not that either party in this interaction necessarily wishes consciously to overpower or destroy the other, but, since the engagement between them takes place at unconscious as well as conscious levels, the forces at work in it are not under the control of the ego. A genie escapes from the bottle and is let loose in the analytic space. What Jung speaks of in this article, but only in the most general terms, is the interactive alchemy that takes place between two people as their psyches become deeply enmeshed. The outcome of this interaction, which he calls transformation, is unpredictable, but he hopes by these means to generate a new sense (on both sides of the therapeutic equation) of individuality and the reorganization of psychic energy around a constellation of the self. The analytic process itself now becomes the pupation stage of psychological metamorphosis, and its end result is an imago.

Some seventeen years later, in 1946, Jung published "The Psychology of the Transference," his definitive statement on the transformative potential of the analytic relationship. In this major essay, he focuses specifically and at length on the fourth stage of analysis—transformation—and offers a far-reaching theory of what takes place psychologically in a transformative relationship. "The Psychology of the Transference" is divided into two parts, the first a general theoretical section and the second an interpretation of a series of alchemical pictures from the *Rosarium Philosophorum,* a medieval text, which Jung uses to illustrate and develop his thesis. The most essential point to grasp, in my opinion, is his observation that four factors are in play in the two-person relationship: the two conscious egos of the people involved (a and b), and two accompanying but highly elusive players, the unconscious figures of each psyche (a' and b'). Moreover, there are relational dynamics actively engaged among all four factors. In other words, there are six couples in a two-person relationship: a to b, a to a', b to b', a to b', a' to b, a' to b'.

In the classic psychoanalytic setup of "only one psyche in the room," the situation appears to be much simpler. The analytically trained ego of the doctor observes the patient's associations and collects observations about the patient's repressed unconscious. These are offered back to the patient in an elucidation of intrapsychic relations (the b to b' couple). There also are interpretations of the relation between the patient's unconscious and the analyst, the classic transference relation (the a to b' couple). But where this view of the relationship falls short is in failing to recognize the mutual unconscious relationship that becomes operative between doctor and patient (the a' to b' couple).

In Jung's much more complicated, but also more complete, modernized version of analysis, this relationship between the unconscious couple not only is recognized, but it becomes the center of attention. At the outset of therapy, the full dimensions of the complex relationship between doctor and patient are not so evident. There is the official professional relationship, the conscious couple, which, as in Freudian analysis and in psychotherapy generally, is established at the beginning of treatment and maintained throughout (the a to b couple). This is regarded as a two-way contract, and each partner takes on certain specific obligations as conscious tasks: the doctor to follow the rules and ethics of the profession and to use all available training and skill for the benefit of the patient; the patient to cooperate with treatment by being as open as possible with the doctor and offering unconscious material as it becomes available in dreams and associations. Meeting time, fees, boundaries, and professionalism dictate the terms of this contract, and the ensuing relationship is contained within this secure framework. This is like the contract drawn up between business partners or the marriage contract between people who want to enter into a marital relationship. It is the first and simplest (if not always the easiest) obligation of the analyst to maintain this relationship and keep it firmly in place at all times during treatment (and perhaps also even after treatment officially has ended). Confidentiality is a rule required by ethics and the law. The official, conscious relationship is the container of analysis, and it is required in order to create trust and safety. Jung, being a proper Swiss and also a highly sensitive and skilled psychotherapist, acknowledged the importance of this conscious relationship.

The classic transference relationship, which takes place between the patient's unconscious and the doctor's ego presentation (the a to b' couple), also is recognized by Jung. This is a half-conscious, half-unconscious couple. The patient's unconscious reacts to the doctor's words and air of authority in a particular way, based upon earlier history and life experience, and from the unconscious come associations to similar figures from the past. There may be a response of immediate and unwarranted trust, even love; conversely, there may be an irrational reaction of fear and suspicion. Both, it is assumed, are based upon previous experiences with authority figures such as parents, guardians, and teachers. Presumably, it was because of this transference dynamic that Breuer's young patient fell in love with the older doctor and impulsively tried to embrace him and kiss him passionately at the end of a session, thus setting off the chain of thought and events that led to Freud's psychoanalysis of the transference. Freud was a master at eliciting and elucidating this relationship, and he made this the centerpiece of, and necessary condition for, psychoanalysis. No transference neurosis, no analysis. Jung deepened the understanding of this relationship by introducing the idea of archetypal transference: the figure of the doctor may be embellished not so much by one's personal father imago (the inner image of one's own father) but rather by a larger-than-life and much more powerful figure like the hero lover, the sage magician, or even God. (Presumably these also were projected upon the personal father in childhood, thus giving him such larger-than-life qualities.)

A similar hybrid couple is constituted in a corresponding dimension between the doctor's unconscious and the patient's conscious presentation, a third couple (the a' to b couple). Jung's early analytic experience augmented the well-trodden psychoanalytic ground of transference with an unruly relationship between his own unconscious and the fascinating presence of his young female patient, Sabina Spielrein. Something about her stirred his poetic soul and entranced him. The psychic factor responsible for this response on his part derived from his own unconscious psyche and was projected onto the patient, young Sabina. This psychological factor was what he would come to call the *anima,* the soul image of the eternal feminine embedded in a man's unconscious.

With this undeniable realization that the doctor could be hooked psychologically by the personality of some patients, not in the parental complexes but in other unconscious centers of desire and potential imago activation, the whole conception of the analytic interaction began to take a new turn. It was not especially surprising that a young doctor could become sexually stimulated and excited by an attractive young female patient, nor was it a cause for wonder that this was considered contamination of the process, something to be rejected before it could interfere with professional treatment. Such would have been the view of Freud, with whom Jung certainly would have agreed on this point. But the deep tenacity of the latter doctor's emotional response, and its seeming meaning for his own psychological development and for his life, called for some rethinking of theory and technique. Perhaps the doctor was in analysis, too; and perhaps this was more of a two-way business than at first had been realized. Certainly Jung no longer was just a neutral listener. He was being drawn by his patients into a mutual play of psyches. And perhaps it was foolhardy—the result of youthful naiveté—that he let himself enter into the relationship with Spielrein and others (not only women but men, too) and allowed himself to be affected by these professional relationships to the extent that he did. But certainly the term *countertransference,* as it then was understood, was a word that did not have much descriptive or explanatory value in these cases. Jung not only was reacting to patients' projections and transferences; he actively was projecting his own unconscious material into them as well. There was a kind of mutual transference going on. From such experiences, Jung would learn a great deal and would vastly change his therapeutic technique and his understanding of the analytic pair.

A fourth couple exists in the relationship between the doctor's conscious ego and unconscious matrix (the a to a' couple). As it is usually described in standard textbooks, countertransference is a result of arousal in this relationship. If the analyst in a particular session becomes unaccountably anxious or emotionally reactive, it usually is taken to be due to some stimulation of a complex in association to something the patient has presented, said, or done. Perhaps a gesture or a phrase of the patient triggers a complex in the analyst's unconscious by association with a parental figure or a scene from childhood. The analyst is trained to monitor this type of reaction and silently analyze it, all the while maintaining composure and facilitating the process under way in the session. Fordham, a leading English analytical psychologist, named this "illusory countertransference."[13] It requires analysis on the therapist's part and often calls for supervisory consultation. This type of emotional reaction on the therapist's part is widely recognized by many schools of psychotherapy and was what Freud and Jung had in mind when they invented the term *countertransference.*

While this is going on in the doctor's psyche, a similar process is occurring in the patient's, making up a fifth couple (the b to b' couple). It is the relationship between the patient's ego and her or his unconscious matrix. Disturbing reactions in response to the doctor's words, office, or physical appearance may arise in the patient's consciousness during a specific session. The rule of analysis is to verbalize these reactions so that they can be examined for their unconscious content. This has been the bread-and-butter of Freudian on-the-couch analysis.

But what had not been recognized by Freud and later was much emphasized by Jung, is another kind of countertransference-transference relation, based upon the relationship between the two unconscious players in the analytic interaction (the a' to b' couple). Since Jung formulated his contribution, this relationship has become the center of much interest and attention in analytical psychology. The entire second part of Jung's essay on the psychology of the transference deals with this dimension of the analytic relationship. To explain the intractability and ultimate unanalyzability of some transferences and countertransferences, and of the relationship that comes into being in the course of long-term therapeutic encounters, Jung had to reflect profoundly and acutely upon the subterranean relationship of unconscious to unconscious. This is an aspect of the relationship that is experienced long before it is, or even can be, analyzed—if indeed it ever is made fully conscious.[14] It is here that we look for images and dynamics that lead to transformation.

As the analytic relationship begins to form at this level of mutual unconsciousness, Jung says, a distinct experience of what he calls "kinship libido"[15] develops. He speaks of a "peculiar atmosphere of family incest."[16] The experienced analyst can detect this mutual affinity and the natural resistances to its recognition and may find evidence of its existence in dreams and associations. What is in the making is the psychic glue that will bond the two partners in this analytic undertaking and hold them in place throughout its duration (and after). This energy of kinship libido attracts and repels the two people in the analytic relationship, and eventually it feeds into the creation of an image based upon a combination of the two psyches involved in this alchemy. This is the transformative image that will contain and guide the pair. It may be brother and sister, father and daughter, mother and son, cousin and cousin, uncle and niece— something with the flavor of a close kinship bond. An irrational union takes place here. A knot is tied.

The *Rosarium* pictures, which Jung uses to depict the development of this mutual image in the unconscious, show a process that begins with a formal meeting, enters a middle phase of intimacy, union, and death, and concludes with the emergence of the imago. It runs its course along the lines of the model I proposed in chapter 1. In the transformative relationship, a caterpillar (larval) stage of becoming acquainted and forming an intimate union is followed by a cocoon (pupa) stage of dormancy, retreat, and seeming death; finally a butterfly (adult imago) stage completes and solidifies the union and gives it permanence.

Both partners in the relationship participate in this transformation, and both enjoy (or suffer) its outcome. Somewhat difficult to grasp and to remember in Jung's written account is the unconsciousness of this process: the entire drama unfolds and plays itself out in the psyche's inner parts, where everything is cloudy and dark and where male may be female, female male, body spirit, and so on. This is not to say that effects of this drama cannot be detected in consciousness, but they are extremely subtle. Equally so is the transformation that slowly takes place in each personality of the therapeutic dyad as the two partners in it encounter one another steadily over an extended period of time.

As Jung describes this transforming interaction, using the *Rosarium* pictures as a guiding thread, the story opens with an image of a sacred space, a fountain (*Rosarium* Series no. 1). This is an image of wholeness that announces the underlying nature and quality of the psychic process to come. It symbolizes a magical space that will contain and nourish the psychic process with its ever-vivifying waters. This is the psychological precondition for a transformative relationship. Such a pregnant moment of maximum opportunity must be constellated, but it also must be recognized that this is beyond the ego's control. Analysis offers a space, formally structured by its ethical rules and boundaries and nourished by the attitudes and values that guide its procedures, but there can be no guarantee that the fountain always will be present.

The fountain, and indeed the whole ensuing process, is presided over and encircled by quite independent archetypal forces and powers—sun, moon, stars—which enclose both analyst and analysand in this mutual undertaking: "The unconscious *spiritus rector* will take over and lead the mind back to the unchangeable, underlying arche-types, which are then forced into projection by this regression."[17] The unconscious is the creator of the relationship that is about to begin; it is present at the beginning, the middle, and the end of the process. And the unconscious is unpredictable.

The transformative relationship itself, which begins in the second picture of the *Rosarium,* starts with a left-handed handshake (*Rosarium* Series no. 2). The meeting of the left hands indicates that the two *unconscious* players of the drama are coming into contact. This signals a pregnant moment of irrational recognition, each of the other, felt as an unusual and surprising sort of openness to a stranger, trust being granted without need of evidence or proof, easy familiar-ity, confidence. It is a moment of massive but hidden projection, suffused with archetypal fantasies and a profound longing for union. This moment also is graced by a sign of transcendence. In the *Rosarium* picture, a dove joins in blessing the relationship that is forming between a King and a Queen as they shake left hands; in therapy, this sign may be an impressively symbolic initial dream or a synchronis-tic event. (In one instance—not in analysis—it was mutual surprise at seeing, suddenly and without forethought or preparation, a full moon hovering above a city skyline.) This marks the beginning of a timeless relationship that will endure through time. The paths of two lives have crossed, and the meeting is momentous.

The images of the *Rosarium* that follow upon this initial meeting depict the gradual development of a love relationship between the King and Queen. There is the moment of full self-disclosure when they face one another naked (*Rosarium* Series no. 3), followed by their entry into a bath (no. 4). They enjoy coitus (no. 5), and from that moment onward they are shown as united in one body (no. 6). A profound merger of unconscious psyches rapidly has taken place; the two have become one. From this new conjoint body, a tiny infant, their mutual soul, emerges (*Rosarium* Series no. 7); but tragically it flies away into the sky. Without a soul, the body now lies lifeless and inert, as though laid out in a tomb. The couple now has entered the darkest moment of pupation. The relationship, having passed through the phases of self-disclosure, intense bonding, blissful union

Rosarium *Series no. 1*

in a warm bath of mutual unconsciousness, and fertilization, enters a phase of depression. There is a crisis of faith. Will this turn out badly? Is this relationship going to end in loss of soul rather than transformation? Or is this loss of soul a prerequisite for the coming transformation?

Analyses go through this sort of crisis, and so do many deeper nonanalytic relationships. Many relationships founder upon this rock. After an initial period of sudden regression, archetypal projections occur that create symbols of transformation and lead to the

Rosarium *Series no. 2*

giving and receiving of inspiration and energy.[18] A union takes place, hope surges, there is a birth of new being, and the unconscious responds with magical assistance and fertile imagination. Then nothing! All is quiet. In fact, it is deathly quiet. What gives? Is it over? Did we make it all up? Or is there something that endures but is quiescent for a time, catching its breath? On the surface, life may go on as before, with routines in place, conventional exchanges, even the im-

Rosarium *Series no. 3*

portant daily therapeutic work of elucidation and education continuing unhampered. But the deeper energies are missing; the instinct that drove the process has vacated. There is no movement. The feeling tone is flat or depressed. For especially sensitive people, this can reach a state of acute depression and anxiety and lead to withdrawal Jung even warns of potential psychosis in connection with feelings of abandonment.[19] In this period of crisis, one may see desperate

Rosarium *Series no. 4*

attempts to jump-start the relationship again, or acting out—by prescribing medication or meditation, introducing new techniques, or entertaining thoughts of changing analysts. The pupa becomes worried; in the darkness of the cocoon, it fears that it is buried there for keeps.

While this is a predictable phase in transformative relationships, it is always a dreadful one. Again, it is a *katábasis,* a dark night of the

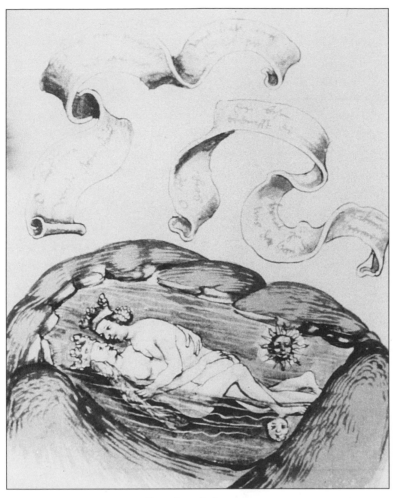

Rosarium *Series no. 5*

soul, and it is most productive—and tolerable—when its presence and reality can be jointly acknowledged. In the conscious relationship of ego to ego, there can be talk about the felt deadness in the relationship. Of course, the analyst risks some "authority"—the illusion of possessing constant and sure knowledge of what is going on, how long it will take, what will come of it—if he or she admits mutuality in this darkness.[20] In many facets of the relationship, things are

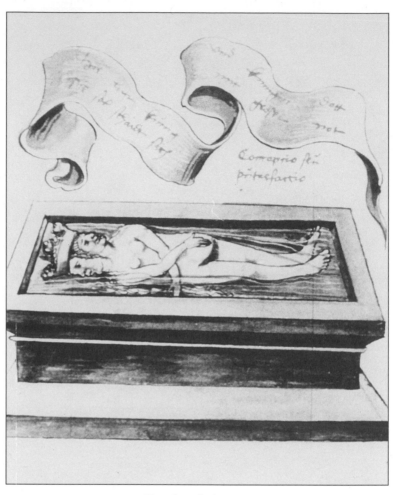

Rosarium *Series no. 6*

much more knowable, even if not always crystal-clear; but for the unconscious couple, all is *Deo concedente* ("God willing"). The only approach is patience, mindfulness, and *wu wei*[21] (the Taoist term for nonjudgment and neutral but keen attentiveness to what is happening). Fordham, following the thought of Bion, says that this involves faith.[22] The eighth illustration in the *Rosarium* Series shows a sign of hope: it is raining.

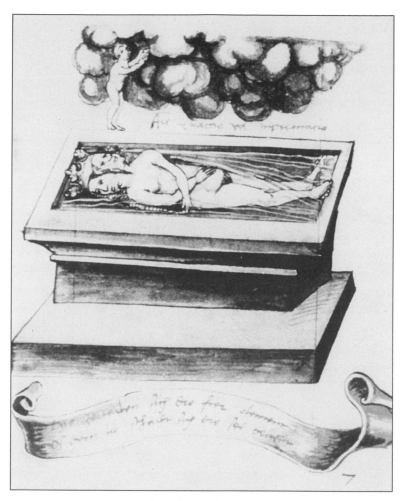

Rosarium *Series no. 7*

According to the *Rosarium,* preparation is now under way in the pupa for a new manifestation as imago. What we have seen up to this point in the *Rosarium* pictures is preparation for what is to come—namely, the Rebis. In the ninth illustration, the soul returns from up yonder and reenters the united body, and this leads to a resurrection or rebirth and to what we can refer back to Jung's notion of deification. The Rebis (*Rosarium* Series no. 10) is an image of archetypal

Transformative Relationships (93)

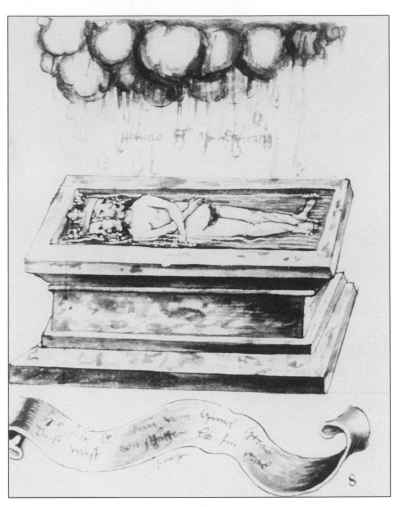

Rosarium *Series no. 8*

unity. When the conjoint body rises from the tomb, it reassumes some of the paraphernalia of royalty—a crown, a pair of scepters—which had been put aside during the bath. Still naked, it bestrides the moon and bears the wings of an angel. This is an image of culmination in the alchemical opus. All of alchemy is about transformation—of lead into gold, *prima materia* into the *lapis,* the instinctual body into the spiritual body.

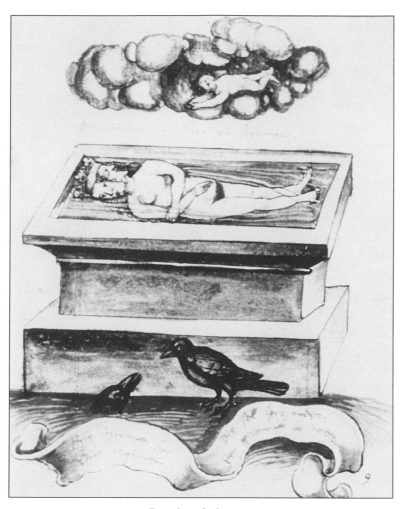

Rosarium *Series no. 9*

In the *Rosarium,* the transformation of two separate objects into one complete unity is depicted by the Rebis. Two become one, and they create a third being, who at first separates from them and then returns and is reabsorbed. Now the Rebis appears. The Rebis symbolizes a realized union of the opposites masculine and feminine. It is the "fourth" in this series. As a deity, the Rebis, like Aion, holds the opposites together in a single image of unity and wholeness: "What

Rosarium *Series no. 10*

the alchemist tried to express with his Rebis and his squaring of the circle, and what the modern man also tries to express when he draws patterns of circles and quaternities, is wholeness—a wholeness that resolves all opposition and puts an end to conflict, or at least draws its sting. The symbol of this is a *coincidentia oppositorum* which, as we know, Nicholas of Cusa identified with God."[23]

In a transformative relationship, an experience of the archetypal self becomes available to both partners through the symbolic object that forms between them. It seems that human nature is such that the activation of transformative images often (perhaps most frequently) occurs between two people (or more) who are joined intimately at deep unconscious levels. Out of this common psychic matrix arises the imagination that generates symbols which not only bind the pair together for life and through generations, but also offer them access to the archetypal basis of psychological life itself. The fountain of living water from picture no. 1 returns as a wellspring of imagination which fertilizes the union and transforms both people in it.

While such symbols of the archetypal self arise spontaneously between people engaged in a transformative relationship, they belong to neither one of them. Actually, they belong to no one. They are archetypal images that dwell in the collective imagination of humankind. As such they are universal and generally available to everyone, everywhere, anytime. Yet who has not fallen into the illusion of assuming ownership of them? People become possessive of their gods and goddesses. From such "ownership" grows dependence, and thus some analyses become interminable. When either person—analyst or patient—claims or assumes that access to the self is contingent upon indefinitely continuing the analytic relationship as it has been constituted by professional rules and guidelines, the only avenue of escape becomes death itself. Analysis becomes marriage "until death do us part." This confuses the conscious relationship that analysis holds in place throughout formal treatment, and attempts to replace the conscious relationship with the subterranean one. It also leads toward an assimilation of the ego by the self, which for Jung approaches the definition of psychosis, and becomes a *folie à deux*. Instead of relating to the images of the unconscious, one becomes possessed by them; ordinary reality disappears in a haze of delusion: "You are in the society of the gods or, if you will, the lunatic society; you are no longer in human society, for you cannot express yourself."[24] The only way to survive and benefit from a transformative relationship is to recognize a basic rule of abstinence: do not attempt to possess or control the spirit.

In analysis, we have rituals of termination. In life, things are not as neatly packaged. Termination is at once a death and a birth. It ends the relationship between the conscious egos—doctor and patient—decisively. One supposes that, by the time termination is scheduled, many facets of the relationship—the mutual transferences—have been clarified, analyzed, and metabolized to whatever extent is possible, given the structures of the ego complex and its defenses, as well as the nature and degree of pathology characterizing the ego and the personal complexes. Termination typically includes a review of the more memorable features of the analytic experience and an evaluation of what has developed from the start of analysis to the present. It is not unlike that other great leave-taking, death; and, as the moment of departure approaches, the pain of loss and the wrenching emotions surrounding separation can be extreme. But there is also the excitement of liberation and freedom, the pleasure of anticipating flight on one's own and of testing one's newfound wings free of analytic support. In some ways, an analytic termination is less like death than going off to, or graduating from, college.

How is the Rebis relationship—the bond, the kinship found and developed, the experience of union and wholeness, the wellspring of symbolic imagination—affected by termination? Not at all, because it lies beyond the range of the ego's control. The Rebis belongs to eternity. "On many occasions I have observed," Jung writes in his commentary on the Rebis image, "that the spontaneous manifestations of the self ... bring with them something of the timelessness of the unconscious which expresses itself in a feeling of eternity or immortality."[25] Time and space constraints do not apply to this relationship, which continues to exist as a symbolic center available to both (now formally separated) partners at any time and in any place they want to renew contact with it. Some theorists of analysis talk

about "internalization" of the analyst and "transmuting internaliza-
tions" (Kohut) to describe what is left of the analytic relationship
after termination has been completed. Structures of analysis certainly
do remain in place long after formal termination. The inner analyst,
moreover, always remains in place as a figure to consult, in whose
presence one ever again can renew oneself through memory and
imagination and association. At this level, too, the personal bond
never is dissolved; it only becomes invisible and more subtle.

If an angel Rebis has been constellated in the relationship, however, there is much more. Rather than only an internalization of the
analyst or even the analytic relationship, there is the memory of
an enduring archetypal image of union—of the self—that was constellated in the depths of mutual unconsciousness during analysis. As
such, it is as important to the inner life of the analyst as of the patient.
The analyst, too, continues to have access to images of the self that
are constellated in work with patients. And it is this constellation of
the self that works the deepest transformations in both people.

I have used the model of analysis with its six "couples"—or,
rather, six vertices of one highly complex couple—to discuss transformative relationships. I have not by this intended in any way to
imply that the same dynamics and vertices do not enter into other
relationships as well. But in other contexts they usually are not quite
so consciously studied and held separate. Instead, they tend to fuse
explosively in the tempestuous dramas of highly charged emotional
relationships between people who are alternately attracted to and
repelled by each other. Attracted, they seek merger and oneness;
repelled, they desire a great degree of separation and individuality.
Love and hate thus combine in a dance that creates marriages, business partnerships, mass movements of many sorts, and then either
destroys them or fosters some measure of individual development. If
one could analyze these emotionally charged relationships psychologically, one most likely would find the full play of mutual unconsciousness that produces images of wholeness and unity and offers
people the opportunity for transformation. In estimating one's relationships, a possible guideline to measure their transformational
effectiveness and power would be the following: If a relationship gen-

erates a flow of images that deepens and clarifies one's perception of the self as this archetype has entered and shaped one's life, if it crystallizes one's basic feelings and attitudes toward life, if it arouses new fantasies about one's future and reframes one's memories of the past, and if it brings forth a new horizon of meaning and opens new avenues of effort and work, then to that degree it is a transformative relationship. Such relationships are the triggers and the contexts for adult transformation, for the formation of an imago.

It is noteworthy that Jung dedicated his essay on transference to his wife. Whatever his difficulties in marriage may have been—Jung's biographers have duly noted them—he must have found in retrospect that his relationship with Emma was transformative, or he would not have dedicated "The Psychology of the Transference" to her. In fact, the marriage was a deeply bonded, enduring, nearly lifelong relationship for both of them. For many people, marriage is a highly complex and at least potentially transformative relationship. It changes many aspects of people's lives. It rearranges their perceptions of past, present, and future, and it channels energy into directions that typically include home, family, and such mundane things as joint retirement accounts. Inwardly, it changes one's self-definition from "single" to "married." Wedding rings signal this new state of affairs.

A marriage does not become transformative simply by verbalizing the wedding vows, trading rings, cutting the wedding cake, and enjoying a honeymoon together, however. Marriages pass through many phases and crises, and only if an irrational bond grows up between the partners and holds firm as the relationship develops and deepens can one speak of marriage as a transformative relationship. To be transformative, a union must take place not only in the conscious relationship but also in the subterranean levels. In marriage, there is an ego level of relating, which is hard enough to manage and is what marriage counselors tend to focus on when trying to improve communication skills and tolerance. But there is also the level of the deep unconscious. It is fully possible—and not that rare—that a tacit agreement is reached between marriage partners to work out issues on the conscious level while more or less ignoring the other dimensions, to say nothing of the subterranean. This is what Guggenbühl-Craig has called the marriage of well-being rather the marriage of individuation. This can be a good social marriage, but it will not be a transformative relationship.

Marriages that are transformative relationships have the effect of generating irrationally based images of wholeness and unity, which both partners can relate to as essential and vitally important to life's meaning. These are not images of an ideal couple, but images of integration that embody the opposites. The images may be grotesque from a naturalistic viewpoint, as in fact the Rebis is. The mutual image of a particular couple—in itself an impersonal archetypal image of the collective unconscious—is uniquely expressive of the pair's specific relational alchemy. At this level, there are no rights or wrongs. The Rebis may be a brother-sister pair, a mother-son pair, or a father-daughter pair. It simply is what it is and what it has to be. Nor are the partners here any longer two separate individuals; they are one, like Siamese twins. They share a single heart. In their egos and conscious adaptation to the world, and in their personas and complex structures—their heads, their upper stories, their personal history—they may be (indeed, they usually are and should be) two unique, very different individuals with separate interests, hobbies, careers, passions. But at the level of the Rebis, they are one in a way that they probably cannot articulate. An irrational bond exists. Here there is a winged being, a Rebis, who is neither of them and yet both of them.

In a transformative relationship, the Rebis is not a static image or an object, like an idol, to worship and propitiate. It is a vital presence, the spirit of the union, the irrational foundation of the joint enterprise. It can be seen in the aura that surrounds a pair. It is the source of their joint energy and vitality as a couple. What has transpired through the relationship is that the *spiritus rector,* who brought the couple together in the first place—through an improbable accident, a synchronistic event, a chance encounter—and blessed them with the gift of instant recognition and a flow of kinship libido, now is absorbed into the ongoing relationship. The Rebis is winged, a spirited background presence, the particular atmosphere and aroma of a couple. It is the source of the intuitive foreknowledge which allows one to anticipate the words and thoughts of the other, the psychological factor which sends one of them dreams which pertain to the other as well, the unconscious link connecting the couple's timing even when they are far apart. The Rebis is bound by neither time nor space. And it survives the absence or even the death of a partner, maintaining the relationship beyond the seemingly final limit of the grave.

In his late-life memoir, *Memories, Dreams, Reflections*, Jung reports two dreams that illustrate this permanence of the marriage bond. The first is somewhat humorous. He tells of a dream he had in 1922 when he was in his mid-forties, some twenty-five years after his father's death. In it, his father comes to him for marriage counseling. Paul Jung had been informed that his son was a knowledgeable psychologist, and he wanted to consult him about marital psychology. As Carl began to prepare a lecture on the complexities of marriage, he suddenly awoke and was surprised to have had this unusual dream. Shortly thereafter, his mother died unexpectedly. "My dream was a forecast of my mother's death, for here was my father who, after an absence of twenty-six years, wished to ask a psychologist about the newest insights and information on marital problems, since he would soon have to resume this relationship again."[26] In Carl's unconscious, at least, the marriage bond between his father and mother was permanent and still intact after twenty-six years of separation by death. The synchronistic connection between his dream and his mother's death bears a mysterious witness to the enduring tie.

Similarly, Jung had a dream of his own wife, Emma, after her death. At that point, he was in his late seventies and had been married to her for fifty-three years. By all accounts, his marriage, like his father's, had been a difficult one, yet it had been a vital and deeply meaningful relationship throughout his adult life. Certainly it had been a transformative relationship, as well as a containing one, for both partners. Jung writes that his wife appeared to him as in a portrait, dressed in her beautiful original wedding gown, which was designed and created by Jung's cousin, Helene Preiswerk. Emma faced him squarely, and her expression indicated the wisdom of acceptance and objectivity. She was beyond emotion. The portrait, he says, summed up their whole relationship. "Face to face with such wholeness one remains speechless, for it can scarcely be comprehended,"[27] he writes about this final image of Emma. This dream exemplifies the timeless transcendence of the bond, a Rebis that joins the partners in a symbolic unity. The dream pictures an imago that both Carl and Emma incarnated as their years together advanced. They shared a wisdom imago.

The Rebis bond in a transformative relationship continues to work its effects over the long course of time. It is what creates the underground spaces in a relationship, as depicted in the dream I quoted at the beginning of this chapter. While it is the ground and basis for the relationship, it is also the channel via which the dynamic power of the unconscious continuously recreates the relationship and the partners in it. Relationships often are seen as containers for people—the "container" and the "contained" is how Jung describes the two partners in a marriage[28]—but they are equally transformers if they constellate the Rebis factor. The relationship becomes the dynamic factor that changes both people in the direction of a mutual image of integration and wholeness. It is an image that holds conscious and unconscious, masculine and feminine, good and bad, in a frame of joined polarities. It is not a matter of one partner becoming inclined to be more like the other, but rather of both coming to approximate a shared image of wholeness. In Jung's case, he and Emma shared what can be called a "wisdom imago," which also was an outgrowth of Jung's earlier Aion experience. This means that both he and Emma developed and deepened, during the second half of life, toward a realization of the self that took its primary cues from religion and philosophy. For a couple of artists, the imago would be tilted in the direction of art and aesthetics; for a couple of scientists, it would emphasize the features of knowing and understanding.

The reason old married partners look so much alike and share so many values, attitudes, and behavior patterns is that they have been unconsciously guided in the same direction by a joint imago. This has not been imposed on one by the other, unless one of them has an exceptionally dominant personality. Rather, it has grown up in both of them from below, so to speak, from the Rebis that has formed out of the union of their unconscious psyches. It is this factor that transforms them over the course of a long span of life together, often until it becomes difficult to tell one from the other, so close do both now approximate their common imago.

This sort of transformative process also underlies and guides whole kinship groups, communities, and collective movements. Communities of nuns who live together for years under the spiritual presence and direction of a powerful founder unite through an imago that unites their personalities through unconscious mergers and identifications. The founder may be the magnet drawing them into this communal imago, although her individual character and personality may remain unique and distinct from those of her followers. But as they take on similar features of attitude and behavior, even of physical appearance, a common Rebis image constellates and can be detected beneath the surface. As a unit, they portray an imago of the collective unconscious. The Amish, whose personalities are immersed from birth to death in collectively shared values and attitudes, achieve imagos (adult forms) that are nearly identical psychologically. The transformation that shapes an individual life from birth and youth into its adult imago depends upon the constellation of a transformative image out of the depths of the collective unconscious; in the case of tightly woven communities, this constellation is anything but unique and individual. It is collective and narrowly restricted by the group, and that is the aim: to produce adults who in their mature adult imagos match markings and colors to the greatest extent possible. The individual has to struggle mightily to separate from these magnetic communities, and even when this is done, the adult imago often still resembles the traditional one.

What I have argued in this chapter is that imago formation also takes place within the context of a two-person relationship, if the latter goes deep enough to constellate a Rebis. When that happens, the couple supplants the community in shaping the mature adult imago. In modern times, with the general breakdown of large communities, families, and marriages, the relationship developed in psychotherapy sometimes becomes the most significant transformative relationship in an adult's life. The Rebis constellated by the analytic pair has helped to shape contemporary notions of maturity and adulthood. Analysis has been a relational context in which the spirit of transformation has been invoked and welcomed. The result may be the constellation of an image of adult maturity that is different from traditional images. Perhaps it is this image that will shape and define what it means to be a fully ripened adult human being in the future: not *homo religiosis* but *homo psychologicus.*

CHAPTER 4

Three Portraits of Transformation: Rembrandt, Picasso, Jung

> The secret of alchemy was . . . the transformation of
> personality through the blending and fusion of the
> noble with the base components, of the differentiated
> with the inferior functions, of the conscious with the
> unconscious.
>
> —C. G. Jung

Listening to a Beethoven symphony or string quartet, it is hard to refrain from believing that the composer was born specifically to give the world this music. Is there not a Master's hand at work in such manifestations of spirit in human life? The beauty and astonishing variety of butterflies is matched by the splendor and generous abundance of forms taken by the human imago. God *must* be an artist.

Yet, I say to myself, this sounds awfully pre-Darwinian. Arguing from artifact to artificer went out with eighteenth-century Deism. This type of argument is out of fashion in this scientistic age. We do not *know*,[1] in a way that can be scientifically verified or subjected to empirical study, if there is a Designer behind the design. All we can allow ourselves as moderns to observe is that there are people who accept the challenge when angels call, and when transformative images and opportunities for life fall unannounced into their lives. They engage these synchronicities creatively, and through this interaction they transform themselves and constellate their adult psychological imagos. But no more than caterpillars ask for moltings or metamorphosis do transformative persons consciously invite these crises and pivotal relationships into their lives. Nor do they choose the final form of the imago. The periods of deepest transformation often are lived as dark nights of the soul. There is no evidence of things to come. This is the pupation phase in the evolution of an imago whose design is beyond conscious intention.

Having discussed (in chapter 1) the process of transformation in the middle of life, argued (in chapter 2) that transformation takes place by means of transformative images, and described (in chapter 3) one of the contexts in which adult transformation occurs—the intimate relationship—I now come to this last chapter with an urgent desire to communicate the freedom and delightful creativity offered by the psychological imago. Again I invoke the image of the butterfly.

This account offers greatly condensed biographies of three supremely gifted individuals whose lives exemplify transformation and fully realized imago formation. My hope is that these capsule portraits will suggest how the innate imaginal disks buried within the personality are drawn forward and knit together to achieve full capacity in the adult individual's conscious attitudes and activities, and how the resultant imago then reflects and guides a person's destiny in the second half of life.

When the psychological self—the adult imago—is constituted and fully realized in the second half of life, a person acquires with it the freedom to expand and deploy the expression of psychic energy in a distinctive and highly creative way.[2] The imago opens new vistas, while it also defines the individual's psychological style. It brings this capacity to the personality because it draws together the most important opposites in the individual psyche—the high and the low, the sacred and the profane, the conscious and the unconscious—into a singular pattern. The imago is an internal structure made up of psychic polarities, and therefore it often is represented as something grotesque and unrefined from a naturalistic point of view, like the Rebis. But this very lack of conscious polish and perfection gives it the capacity to embrace and channel enormous vitality, and to function as a guiding, releasing, and orienting symbol. The formation of the imago is the precondition for full adult freedom to be oneself and to become the person one most deeply longs to be. Constraints imposed by an earlier persona formation, by social and psychological limits placed upon the individual by a psychosocial identity, are largely surmounted through the active presence of the imago. With this symbolic formation, a personality becomes free to experience and to express a much greater degree of inherent wholeness than was possible previously. The imago is equivalent to adult integrity, and, as John Beebe implies in his book *Integrity in Depth*, integrity transcends character (though it does not abolish it). I see this kind of expanded freedom—to imagine and to exercise innate gifts within the framework of a distinctive style—in the three figures under consideration in this chapter.

I have chosen three people whose biographies, I believe, demonstrate a fully formed imago and, as a result of it, integrity within a transformed personality: Rembrandt van Rijn, Pablo Picasso, and Carl Jung. These three men certainly do not qualify as saints or unblemished heroes, but in each case, while problematical character structures remain evident throughout the second half of life, the adult imago functions to express and orient the manifestations of psychic energy. While the imago transcends character, it does not abolish it or change its fundamental features. It adds another dimension to the psyche.

I have chosen these figures as exemplars not because I believe they represent high moral or spiritual ideals but because each undeniably achieved a sharply distinctive imago. All three lived remarkably creative and fairly long lives and left behind concrete evidence of the transformation process and its net result in their works. The painters Rembrandt and Picasso deposited a detailed record of their transformation processes in their works of art and especially in their self-portraits, and Jung left a written account of personal transformation and a physical monument to his wholeness in the stone tower he built at Bollingen. Because their processes were externalized in artistic images and written works that are publicly available, they lend themselves to study and reflection. While their lives obviously differed in many ways, these men have in common vividly limned adult imagos which both defined them and freed them to express their psychic potential.

I chose these three figures, too, because, among other things, they offer sufficient contrast and differences to avoid the presumption that all transformation processes must culminate in the same type of imago. Human imagos are as varied as butterflies. One could multiply examples almost endlessly, but limitations of time and space forced me severely to limit my selection. I considered including a woman—Eleanor Roosevelt came to mind as a prime candidate for study, as did Georgia O'Keefe and Frieda Kahlo—but I decided instead to use the historical contrast between traditional imago (Rembrandt) and modern (Picasso and Jung).

These biographical vignettes are intended simply as illustrations, it should be emphasized again; in no way do I mean to suggest them as ideals or models to be emulated. Each man can be seen as limited by his own character structure, historical period, and culture, but each also grew beyond these limitations and embodied an imago of archetypal, transcendent dimensions. These are three examples of deification, in Jung's sense of the term, yet they are radically different from one another. Different gods yield different imagos. While we can affirm that all gods ultimately are One, the concrete manifestations are many, and plurality is what confronts us when we look at the world empirically.

Rembrandt van Rijn was born in Leiden on July 15, 1606, and lived his entire life of sixty-three years in seventeenth-century Holland. His father, Harmon Gerritszoon van Rijn, was a miller who had converted to Calvinism; while his mother, Cornelia Willemsdochter van Suyttbroeck, remained Roman Catholic. Rembrandt was the eighth of nine children in a traditional middle-class Dutch family. He was the only one of his siblings to take up an artistic career, an individual decision on his part. His father sent him to the University of Leiden at the age of fourteen to study law, but after a few months he left and apprenticed himself to a Leiden painter named Van Swenenburgh. While Rembrandt must have been at least somewhat literate, no written records or texts from his hand are available. What is known about him is contained in several early biographies and in records of his professional and financial dealings. More important, we can read the development of his inner life from his masterful paintings. Already in the paintings of his youth, he shows a vital, lively, adventurous personality. He had astonishing natural talent. Quickly he outstripped his masters, demonstrating the brilliant flair for dramatic gesture and expression that would characterize his work throughout his life.

Many books have been written about Rembrandt's life and paintings. I will draw on some of them but do not propose here to review them or to duplicate their efforts. What I am interested in is looking at his work—particularly his self-portraits—for evidence of psychological transformation and imago formation. The general stages of his psychological development can be read in his self-portraits. They reveal what Rembrandt saw when he looked in the mirror, what he wanted his audience to see in the way of a maturing and mature European painter of his day, and, to the psychologically trained eye, what was transpiring in his psyche as he grew and then metamorphosed into the imago he was to become.

In the course of his life, Rembrandt drew, etched, or painted his self-portrait approximately one hundred times. He began creating images of himself early on. Using himself as a model, he experimented with expression, light and dark contrast, and clothing. There are many images of him as a young man. In some of these he is scowling, or frowning, or snarling; in others he is dressed as a dandy, a nobleman, a blade about town. Occasionally he paints himself in historical costume as a distinguished noble or exotic prince. Although Rembrandt never traveled physically outside Holland, his imagination roamed far and wide, and he tried on many imaginative personae. He was showing the many sides of his emerging young personality as well as his formidable skill as a portrait painter.

Meanwhile, he enjoyed early success as a fast-rising star in the world of art. Holland's economy was booming, its freedom from Spain recently having been won, and wealthy middle-class merchants and their families were generating a strong demand for paintings of all kinds to decorate their well-stocked Amsterdam houses. After Rembrandt moved from Leiden to Amsterdam in 1630 at the age of twenty-four (the same year his father died), his career took off, and by 1632 he was numbered among the famous in his newly adopted city. His grand historical and biblical paintings were popular among the prosperous burghers of Amsterdam, and his portraits of citizens and their wives and children commanded good prices.

In June 1634, Rembrandt married Saskia Uylenburgh, an intelligent and literate young woman who, though an orphan, brought a dowry of forty thousand guilders, a handsome fortune at the time. With this money the couple bought a large house in Sint Anthonies-dijk, a respectable area of the city, and there Rembrandt set up his studio and with Saskia lived the life of a proper middle-class citizen. A famous painting from this period, entitled *Self-Portrait with Saskia* (1636), shows the painter holding Saskia on his lap, both of them dressed in gorgeous finery and the husband wearing a boldly feathered hat and a prominent sheathed sword. According to commentators, he is proposing an audacious toast to his audience, in rebuttal to charges that he was wasting Saskia's money. At this stage of his life—age thirty—Rembrandt was rather full of himself and more than a little inflated with his own powers and importance. His considerable worldly success gave him grounds for feeling self-confident. He was established.

Unexpectedly and tragically, after giving birth to Titus (the only one of their three children to live beyond infancy), Saskia died in 1641, and a new chapter opened in Rembrandt's life. At thirty-five, he was close to what would be the exact midpoint of his life. He was at the peak of his public celebrity and recognition, but things soon were to change. Though he was still surrounded by students, commissions began to dry up because other younger artists were pursuing new styles and genres, and these were gaining in popularity. Never one to adjust his artistic preferences to current fashion, Rembrandt saw his income decline. His remarkable genius, though still recognized, diminished in commercial value, and his character turned troublesome and stubborn. Clients complained of his tendency to please himself rather than adapt his work to their desires, and Calvinist Amsterdam frowned hard when it became known that he had begun an intimate relationship with a young housemaid, twenty years younger than himself, named Hendrickje Stoffels.

Beautiful portraits of Hendrickje—as a woman in elegant furs, smiling subtly like Mona Lisa; as Bathsheba at her bath; as a voluptuous young woman lifting her dress and bathing in a stream; as a dark and richly dressed woman peering out of windows, with a totally black room behind her—grace this period of Rembrandt's artistic output and indicate his profound grasp of her meaning, for him, as an image of the eternal feminine, the anima. There could be no more beautiful testimony to a man's intense anima experience at midlife than that found in Rembrandt's paintings of Hendrickje. In the portraits of Saskia, he depicted a lively and attractive wife who showered wealth and love and support on her heroic young spouse; in those of Hendrickje, he shows the transformative anima image, the woman who takes a man into dark, unexplored waters of the psyche. Rembrandt followed her with characteristic abandon.

By 1656, Rembrandt was bankrupt financially. He was fifty years old. Most of his belongings were sold off to pay debts, and ownership of his house had to be transferred to his son, Titus. Students of Rembrandt's self-portraits comment on the irony of his great painting of 1658, in which the artist depicts himself seated in regal splendor, a Jovian image with scepter held lightly in his left hand, presenting to the world an image of golden success and middle-aged prosperity. Materially, nothing could have been further from the truth. Psychologically, however, he was not faking. He was painting the portrait of an imago, of the fully realized artist. This is a representation not of a worldly persona, but of an inner truth. Rembrandt was at the height of his powers as an artist and as a man. His brilliant dark eyes look out at the viewer with piercing intensity. He challenges anyone to question his authority. The firm mouth and set jaw reveal none of his worldly troubles or financial circumstances. Not defiant, he

Rembrandt, Self-Portrait, *1658. Courtesy The Frick Collection, New York.*

simply carries his years with authority and supreme dignity. It is the image of a man in the prime of his adult life, for all the world a master and a king. This is the culmination of his development as a distinguished public painter of his times, a man of great worth and stature. In this self-portrait, Rembrandt represents himself as a fully realized artist with the personal authority and freedom to execute his will absolutely and to spend his capital of psychic energy as he sees fit. No one else will dictate style or content to such a master of his own house.

After this, however, Rembrandt's self-portraits change dramatically in style and tone. He has entered another phase of inner development, which we can conceptualize as further deepening and enriching the imago we see in the self-portrait just described. In addition, it represents a dramatic extension of certain features of that imago, as the artist grows into what will be for him old age. As he takes up this last phase of his life—he will live to be only sixty-three—the trappings and aura of pomp disappear, and another distinctive image begins to come forward. It is this archetypal imago that will carry him to the end and give his late paintings their spiritual quality.

Throughout his career, Rembrandt was a painter of impressive religious images. Biblical scenes were one of his stocks in trade. He became famous for them. In some, he included himself as one of the characters in the scene. In late life, though, a shift occurs, and his work becomes more personal and highly realistic. The self-portraits begin to depict his face and hands with graphic realism. Wrinkles, jowls, a bulbous nose, gray hair become apparent. The age of idealized persona presentation and self-promotion now is behind him. He no longer emphasizes the ego. The dramatic costume no longer is his prop. In these late paintings, we find a simple, rather unattractive old man, but light, signaling inner illumination, begins to emanate from his forehead, in striking contrast to the evidence of creeping physical decay and decrepitude. He is extending his imago into the spiritual dimension while recognizing the physical ravages of age.

In the *Self-Portrait,* c. 1661–62, Rembrandt once again depicts himself as an artist. He is wearing a simple white hat and holds his palette and brushes in one hand as he stares soberly ahead. The point of most intense illumination falls on the right side of his forehead. It is as if light were emanating from his head. Obviously he now is a fully mature, even somewhat elderly (the painting was made in his fifty-seventh year), man; if anything, he exaggerates his age. There is

Rembrandt, Self-Portrait, *c. 1661–62. Courtesy The Iveagh Bequest,*
Kenwood House, London.

little trace of narcissistic self-flattery here. The left side of his face is
in shadow, while the hat and his upper forehead are bathed in in-
tensely bright light. The bottom of the painting disappears into total
darkness. The artist here restates his identity as a painter, and he does
this against a background that shows two gigantic circles embedded
in a wall. The circles have been interpreted as a reference to time
itself and as an allusion to a famous artist of antiquity, Appelles, who

reportedly was able to draw perfect circles freehand. The circle also can be taken as an allusion to eternity. As a mandala, it suggests the backdrop of timeless archetypal forms against which the mature painter works in time and space. In this painting, Rembrandt portrays his frail empirical reality proudly in relationship to symbols that transcend time, bringing his human limitations and mundane identity as a workman into connection with the divine. His imago is moving toward a union of opposites—time and eternity. As he looks out upon the world through the eyes of an artist, he is showing himself and the object world in a relation to eternity. This indicates that he is inhabiting a conscious attitude that links the time-bound human body-ego to timeless archetypal images of pure spirit. The light on Rembrandt's head signals what Jung calls deification.

As his position in the world deteriorated socially and economically—Rembrandt in 1660 was forced to move from his house to a more modest dwelling in a neighborhood of artisans and artists—it seems that the sense of gravity and serenity in his paintings increases. It has been noted by students of his work that, toward the end of his life, his painting becomes visionary. In these last years, he continued to paint for the odd commission and to struggle just as stubbornly as ever with his former creditors, who would not leave him in peace and who stubbornly insisted on payment to the last guilder. For the roof over his head and his daily sustenance, he became dependent upon his common-law wife, Hendrickje, and his son, Titus. Four years before his death, he painted a portrait of himself as a sort of old fool. In the self-portrait, he peers out of darkness with an expression of eerie laughter. It is a hard image to read. He may be showing himself as a drunken old fool; more likely, he is laughing with the gods. Again his forehead is brightly illuminated, while much of the picture lies in darkness. The smile is almost a painful grimace, and the stooped shoulders indicate the weight of the burdens he must be carrying. Perhaps this is a holy fool. There is a theory that in this painting he is referring to the Greek artist Zeuxis's death. A story is told that Zeuxis died laughing when an ugly old rich woman paid him a large sum of money and then asked him to paint her as

Rembrandt, Self-Portrait, Laughing. *Courtesy Cologne, Wallraf-Richartz Museum.*

Aphrodite. This reference would imbue the self-portrait with the mirth of the artist who knows sublime beauty and the immense abyss that separates it from human narcissistic grandiosity and desire. The task of the artist, Rembrandt would say, is to paint the truth, not to create flattering images for wealthy customers. Rembrandt was in a brutally honest phase of his life, and human folly surely must have seemed to merit only scornful laughter—the laughter of Zeuxis, another archetypal painter.

As his life entered its final few years, Rembrandt's conditions did not improve. If anything, they worsened. His reputation as a renowned painter provided him little in the way of concrete reward. Yet, in his final self-portraits, he depicts himself as an artist who has joined the company of the immortals, exceeding even such illustrious contemporaries and predecessors as Titan and the Italian masters of the sixteenth and seventeenth centuries, with whom Rembrandt had been competitive throughout his career. On the other hand, these self-portraits are statements of great personal modesty. The artist is brutally honest about his less than ideal physical appearance, yet he shows his figure as illuminated by divine inner light. In the final group of self-portraits, painted in his last years, including one that dates from 1669, the year of his death, Rembrandt repeatedly accentuates the crown of light upon and around his head. In a late masterpiece, he depicts himself as Saint Paul, for Protestant Christians the ultimate image of sanctity and nearness to God. (While Rembrandt is not known to have been an active member of any denomination, it is on the record that he was drawn to Mennonites, who at the time occupied prominent positions in Amsterdam. The inner life of contemplation and piety cultivated by this self-effacing Protestant sect must have appealed to Rembrandt.) Next to Jesus himself, Saint Paul ranked as close as a human could come to integrating fully the presence of God in human form. For Rembrandt to paint himself as Saint Paul was as near as he could approach to the idea of deification without falling into absolute sacrilege by claiming identity with Christ or with God Himself. In his *Self-Portrait as the Apostle Paul,* Rembrandt further extends his imago vertically.

One can conclude that Rembrandt pictorially displays in his self-portraits a transformation process that extends through his entire adult life. Beginning with pictorial experimentation, extravagance of gesture, and the drama of exotic costume—the elaborate and playful artifice of the *puer* phase—the images shift into portraits of greater substantiality in his personae as Dutch artist, as lover and husband,

Rembrandt, Self-Portrait as the Apostle Paul. *Courtesy Rijksmuseum, Amsterdam.*

and finally as the fully realized adult man of power and authority. He attains his imago certainly by the time he is fifty years of age. He has become the fully realized personality and artist we know as Rembrandt. Meanwhile, however, from midlife onward, a series of crises in his personal life undermine his worldly position. After the crash of bankruptcy and loss of possessions and home, he enters a final phase of transformation—a further deepening and enriching of his imago. This phase carries him beyond the meaning of all of his earlier self-portraits to images of self-acceptance, integrity, spiritual illumination, and a profound inner realization of the transcendent function—the personal relation between one's time-bound ego reality and the transcendent realm of the archetypes. His last group of self-portraits, painted during the fifteen years before he died, increasingly show images not only of the artist as fully realized and in masterful command of his materials, but also of the man Rembrandt as a fully realized spiritual being. As one commentator points out, in these late paintings it is "as if the painter were merging into his painting."[3] Using the specific images and the notions available in seventeenth-century Amsterdam, Rembrandt depicted the process of psychological transformation as the emergence of an archetypal imago that combined the vocation of the artist and the spiritual illumination of the saint.

The imagos that people realize in their individual development are based on archetypal forms which, while themselves relatively timeless and unchanging from age to age, nevertheless are shaped and conditioned by history and culture as they find actual expression. As we jump forward from the seventeenth to the twentieth century, we discover in Pablo Picasso an artistic imago different in some obvious respects from that of Rembrandt, but one nevertheless grounded in the archetypal figure of the creative artist.

An artist arguably as talented as Rembrandt was, Picasso in some ways was the obverse of Rembrandt in terms of psychological and spiritual development. These two men were separated by a couple of centuries, and enormous changes occurred in European culture during that time. One factor that complicates this comparison, of course, is that so much more is known about Picasso's life than is available on Rembrandt's. The profusion of detail can have the paradoxical effect of obscuring rather than illuminating major transformational themes. One can miss the forest by concentrating on the fascinating trees. Picasso's love life and his relationships with wives and mistresses, for example, have received a disproportionate amount of attention. This is important information, in that he did become himself in part through these intimate relationships; but it also can be misleading, if his poor interpersonal skills become the main focal point. Character becomes so highlighted that one cannot any longer see the imago. If we look at imago formation—the emergence of the self in adulthood—we find that Picasso, like Rembrandt, achieved a full metamorphosis, but the kind of imago he became is very different from that which Rembrandt embodied. This is true even though both imagos partake of the archetypal form of the creative artist. This difference is the difference between "traditional man" and "modern man."

Modernity is characterized by fragmentation and loss of a unified center of identity. The center does not hold, as Yeats worried, and the psyche is experienced as dis-integrated. To survive, psychological dissociation has become essential. Picasso's art, which breaks whole images into pieces and abstracts objects and then reassembles them into a novel form, is the key to the modern experience. This is what it means to be modern. That is why Picasso is the artist of the century. He gives this experience of fragmentation, dissociation, and loss of soul its most blatant expression. The traditional person demonstrates a more or less straight individuation trajectory. It encompasses a prolonged metamorphosis at midlife and arrives at a distinctly spiritual imago in old age; witness Rembrandt. The modern person's life, on the other hand, typically reveals many attempts at consolidation, a pattern of continual self-deconstruction and attempted reintegration, and often a final ironic statement about anxiety and emptiness. The intervals between intense cultural effort (i.e., work) are filled with physical gratification and/or addictions, while ultimate value is placed upon commercial success or individual creativity for its own sake. This is the collective tone of modernity, and it characterizes Picasso's life.

The question is: can one speak at all of transformation, deification, and imago formation in the context of chaotic and narcissistic modernity? Only if we look deeper. There we may find the archetypal outlines of imago formation and resolution. For this, too, Picasso is a prime case study. If Rembrandt moves from darkness to light and realizes deification in the imago of the archetypal painter-as-apostle (as Saint Paul), what can we see in Picasso's process of transformation?

Picasso, throughout his adult life, was a person in perpetual creative movement. Richardson notes:

> Picasso liked to mark important anniversaries by doing a painting which would signify a change in his work as well as in his life. Around the time of his twenty-fifth birthday (October 19, 1906), he executed a group of self-portrait paintings and drawings, which . . . unveil a totally new Picasso: a sunburned Dionysos in an undershirt, his hair *en brosse*, all set to challenge and subvert the tradition of European art up to and including Cézanne, whose self-portrait had partly inspired this image. How cool, how laconic the artist looks, before he embarks on his messianic mission.[4]

According to no less standard an authority than the *Encyclopedia Britannica*, "While other masters such as Matisse or Braque tended to stay within the bounds of a style they had developed in their youth, Picasso continued to be an innovator into the last decade of his life."[5] His output was prodigious. At his death, he still retained in his personal collection some fifty thousand of his own works from all the periods and in all the styles and media of his lengthy career as an artist.

Picasso is considered to be one of the most transformative figures in all of art history. With a few artist cohorts, he changed the direction of Western art decisively, and "virtually no twentieth-century artist could escape his influence."[6] While Rembrandt perhaps painted better than anyone before or after him, Picasso changed the course of painting itself, like some mighty Hercules redirecting the flow of a major river from an ancient bed into an entirely new one. This is the very definition of transformation: to shift the flow of energy radically from one channel, one form or metaphor, into another. The total quantum of psychic energy poured by humankind into artistic expression—whether painting, drawing, sculpture, or ceramics—

may not have changed as a result of Picasso's labors, but the forms that contain and express this energy have been altered utterly. Picasso was a transformer on a vast collective level. Of course, it must be recognized, too, that he was expressing the *Zeitgeist*. He was able to rechannel Western art in this way because the changes going on in the collective life of the West were reflected in this art. Perhaps it would be more accurate to say, then, that Picasso's gift was to be deeply attuned to the times and to develop and elaborate a style of art that perfectly reflected them. Art changed because culture was changing, and Picasso was one of the chief innovators expressing this change.

If we consider Picasso's artistic production from the viewpoint of his own personal psychological evolution over the course of his long creative life (he was born in 1881 and died in 1972, a span of ninety-one years), we can find a wealth of evidence to support the notion of transformation and imago formation. There are many youthful moltings in the first half of life that begin and end his famous "periods": the Blue Period, the Pink Period, the Cubist Period, etc. Each period is a significant manifestation of the young Picasso, and each plays its part in preparing for the following stages, until an adult imago finally is achieved. After midlife these moltings cease. There are no more distinctive, extended stylistic periods. In the second half of life, Picasso uses many styles. He changes styles of painting constantly, breaking old molds, inventing new ones, and ranging over the entire spectrum from classical and representational to abstract. But he does not remain committed to any one of them beyond an individual work. His imago as an artist now transcends style and technique. Style no longer dictates how he will paint or sculpt or etch; rather, his artistic ego moves freely from one style to another as mood or occasion demands. Picasso, now the complete artist, moves freely and with creative abandon, like a butterfly, among all the media and styles available to him.

One can compare the psychological development evident in Picasso's self-portraits to that seen in Rembrandt's, but the usefulness of doing so is limited. Picasso, too, was a masterful painter of his own image, but his explicit self-representations are rather limited in number and do not extend beyond his youth (except for those done at the very end of his life, to be discussed later). Much like Rembrandt in his early self-portraits, though to my mind less flamboyant and cosmopolitan, Picasso in these paintings plays with images of himself, experimenting with his appearance by dressing up in different costumes, by grimacing, by role-playing and modeling himself to himself. He is trying on identities, wearing them for a while, and then discarding them. To quote John Richardson, he shows himself as "a romantic vagabond, a glamorous *jeune premier*, a decadent poet, a top-hatted dandy and much else besides."[7] None of these roles fits the young bohemian artist exactly, certainly not permanently, but all show facets and possibilities for a persona. Picasso especially is fascinated with his eyes, a feature that in later works would become a signature item.

After the age of twenty-six, Picasso's own representational image dissolves, reappearing in a multitude of enigmatic references, disguises, and ambiguous self-disclosures. In a sense, all his work now becomes subtly autobiographical, and every portrait can be interpreted partially as a self-portrait. This strategy opened to Picasso a whole new world of possibilities for self-disclosure, subterfuge, ambiguity, and symbolic self-representation. "Picasso often 'inhabited' his creations without any reference to his physiognomy, vesting himself in a bestiary of natural and fanciful creatures, in objects like pipes or doorknobs, and even in patterns (such as varicolored diamonds of the Harlequin's costume) or other abstract signs,"[8] to use Kirk Varnedoe's exquisite wording. This strategy may indicate a keen intuitive grasp on Picasso's part of psychological projection and of the subtle intermingling of subjectivity with representations of the object world. It certainly also communicates a Hermetic identity and a playful cast of mind.

My own impression is that Picasso (much like Rembrandt) quite early in life attained a strong measure of self-confidence and was able to assume a vast array of images without fear of losing touch with his identity. While the ego is not often represented, it is implied throughout the *oeuvre*. There are also, of course, elements of camouflage, denial, self-deception, and defensive distancing in this mercurial elusiveness. Again, this elusiveness of explicit identification is programmatic for the modern person. It is a style that characterizes politicians as well as artists, women as well as men, old as well as young people. It is neither good nor bad; it is simply modern. Depth psychological theory sees the person as made up of multiple centers of consciousness, none of which occupies the central position all the time. Thus, at the core of this theory, the human personality is seen as elusive.

While I cannot possibly offer a complete account of the development of Picasso's full adult imago, I will generalize that the main problem was (as it always is) how to combine the opposites he discovered within himself into a unified, if highly complex, image that would embrace his full reality. An early play of polarities shows itself in a pair of self-portraits from 1901. One of his most significant early statements, *Yo, Picasso* [*I, Picasso*], painted when he was twenty, shows the artist as a handsome Spanish painter with a bright orange-red tie dramatically flaring out above his colorful palette. Strong facial features and prominent piercing eyes indicate the confidence and bravado of the young artist. He could as well be a famous matador, so proud and self-assured is his expression, the set of his jaw, his outward gaze. In the Blue Period, which arrives the same year, we find a contrasting self-portrait that depicts a sallow face, hollow cheeks, eyes sunk back in their sockets, and only the red lips indicating any life at all. The painting's background is an unrelenting blue. The body is covered with an oversized black coat buttoned to the top. It is the image of a vagabond or a suffering contemplative—at any rate a depressive, with a sweet half-smile playing across his features— who is gazing directly at the viewer. To move so quickly from a self-portrait depicting a confident matador-painter to one showing a sickly hollow-cheeked depressive indicates a certain amount of identity confusion—or diffusion—in the young Picasso, before he achieved his more distinctive and adamant imago as an adult man. It is only later, when he has worked through his Blue Period and is able to shed some of the illusions he may have had about himself, that he is able to discover and draw upon a surer and more all-encompassing self-definition.

In 1906, when he paints *Self-Portrait with Palette,* he shows his face, significantly, as a mask. Picasso has discovered the primal qualities of the African mask. He described this important discovery to Malraux:

> The masks weren't just like any other pieces of sculpture. Not at all. They were magic things. But why weren't the Egyptian pieces or the Chaldean? We hadn't realized it. Those were primitives, not magic things. The Negro pieces were *intercesseurs,* mediators; ever since then I've known the word in French. They were against everything—against unknown, threatening spirits. . . . I understood; I too am against everything. I too believe that everything is unknown, that everything is an enemy! Everything! I understood what the Negroes used their sculpture for. . . . The fetishes were . . . weapons. To help people avoid coming under the influence of spirits again, to help them become independent. Spirits, the unconscious (people still weren't talking about that very much), emotion—they're all the same thing. I understood why I was a painter. All alone in that awful museum, with masks, dolls made of the redskins, dusty manikins. *Les Demoiselles d'Avignon* must have come to me that very day, but not at all because of the forms; because it was my first exorcism painting—yes absolutely![9]

Richardson reads the *Self-Portrait with Palette* as triumphant self-affirmation that bears "witness to Picasso's Dionysiac exaltation at this time."[10] As noted earlier,[11] this portrait announces Picasso's challenge to the whole tradition of European art to date. It is also, however, an image that mediates transcendence. It is magic. Picasso has discovered the power of the archetypal unconscious, and he has included this feature importantly in his identity. This is an early appearance of an archetypal imago (the surfacing of an "imaginal disk," if you will), a sort of foretaste of things to come.

In the same year, Picasso made a bold move by painting the face of Gertrude Stein as a mask. When people criticized him for the obvious fact that Gertrude did not look like that, Picasso replied that

Picasso, Self-Portrait with Palette. *Courtesy the Philadelphia Museum of Art.*

someday she would! He was painting an imago before it had fully emerged from the larval stage. This is the face of Gertrude Stein that posterity remembers. It is an archetypal image, her imago. Picasso's strategy in portrait painting can be read as an attempt to capture the noumenal essence beneath the physical surfaces of the phenomenal presentation and thereby to reveal the unconscious structures which

Three Portraits (127)

only a probing intuitive eye can discern and which only the future will manifest more fully.

In 1907 another self-portrait followed, which developed the mask-like face and further "Africanized"[12] it. In this period, Picasso assumed strong leadership in the artistic avant-garde in Paris. He painted one of the most important and revolutionary works in modern art history, *Les Demoiselles d'Avignon* (1907), which also includes a famous mask face placed upon the figure of one of the prostitutes. At this time, he was emerging from a major molting (the Blue Period) with a powerful self-expression of archetypal dimensions. Again like Rembrandt, Picasso put his developing imago in terms of mythic images, which have the capacity to combine physical presence with a strong statement of archetypal transcendence. Besides dazzling Paris, the artist was revealing himself in this image and unearthing the elements of his future imago.[13]

In order to find a vocabulary of images that could represent his forming imago in the fullest possible way, Picasso was forced—by his needs, by his temperament, by cultural circumstances, and by his place in contemporary history—to break free of his Roman Catholic Christian heritage. He had to reach back to the origins of Western culture and even beyond, to the earliest origins of humankind in Africa. The myths of the Greeks and the masks of Africa came to define the imagery that Picasso would deploy to paint his imago as it emerged in the second half of his life. Roman Catholic Christianity, which absolutely ruled his native Spanish culture and also dominated the religious world of his adopted France, was too limited to contain his psyche. It was also, of course, much too identified with a moribund tradition and with right-wing politics to be of any use to the artistic sensibility and psychology of a Picasso. Unlike Rembrandt, Picasso was not spiritually or psychologically contained in a collective religious tradition, and this is what gives his life and work such iconic significance in the twentieth century. They mirror the condition of modern people generally. Picasso would have to find other, non-Christian images and stories to express his contact with the collective unconscious. These he found in Greek myths and African masks. These images allowed him to produce work that was *bien*

couillarde, "ballsy." After discovering African masks and Greek mythology, Picasso would have no problem giving his work "the potency, physicality and heft that the word [*couillarde*] implies."[14]
Vitality and potency—libido—would flow from Picasso's brush as
he embraced these images and worked them into his painting.

In the paintings of the many women who passed into and through
his life, Picasso created an astonishing wealth of images that are a
fusion of the other's reality and the painter's psyche. Who can say
where one begins and the other leaves off—which pieces belong
to Picasso and which to the women? These are neither portraits
nor self-portraits. Picasso was painting at the Rebis level, where the
two personalities mingle and unite in a single image, an alchemical
union. They are "Picasso's women," not in a sense that implies ownership but rather as representations of perceptive and deep psychological experience. For example, in the image of his wife Olga
Khokhlova, he painted his fear of the devouring woman; in the portraits of Marie-Thérèse Walter, his regressive longing to return to the
womb; in portraits of the model in the artist's studio, his engorged
Minotaur passion. In short, these paintings depict the whole range
of his anima moods and his emotional reactions to woman. In them
he also created timeless images by stating their noumenal essences in
color, geometric shape, and abstract symbol. By placing both eyes on
one side of a flat surface, for instance, he shows the whole person,
conscious and unconscious. By accentuating the breasts, the vagina,
the womb, he demonstrates his obsession with sexuality and the essence of the feminine, as this was shared and revealed in the relationships.

Of course, Picasso's perspective is very one-sided and stated entirely from the male point of view. Picasso was palpably masculine. I
do not wish to gloss over the widely publicized problems Picasso had
with women, and they with him, for he was indeed a Spanish male
whose *machismo* was deeply ingrained. Yet the several marriages, the
many liaisons, and the short and longer love affairs did give Picasso
access to the depths of his own soul as he explored his own nature
and many dimensions of relational energy.

The chief icon Picasso arrived at to depict his mature imago was

Picasso, Minotaur image. Courtesy Galerie Berggruem, Paris.

the Minotaur. (A lesser figure was the Faun, another the Monkey.) The use of these part-human, part-animal images as self-representations in many paintings, drawings, etchings, and works in other media constitutes the most extensive artistic expression of his adult imago, the culmination of his inner transformation and his deepest point of contact with the archaic basis of the human psyche. What biblical imagery was for Rembrandt, Greek mythological imagery was for Picasso. Especially in the images of beings half-human and half-animal, and particularly in the figure of the Minotaur, Picasso found figures ample and complex enough to express his full psychological wholeness. I read these as images of the archetypal self. The animal image grounded Picasso in the archetypal.[15]

Remembering Jung's account of "deification" as a symbolic transformation into the figure of Aion, who also was a hybrid being made of a human body and the head of an animal, we should not too quickly assume that Picasso, in the image of the Minotaur, is presenting himself simply as bestial. The Minotaur was a child of Poseidon, Lord of the Sea, and Pasiphaë, Queen in the Creton Palace at Knossos. To discover the image of the Minotaur as a self-image is also to become one with the divine (or at least the semidivine) and to gain access to the creative power and energies of the archaic collective unconscious. Picasso's transformation is not a traditional spiritual one like Rembrandt's, in the sense of enlightenment, higher consciousness, and triumphant transcendence over the vicissitudes of the physical and material world. There is no evidence of achieved serenity in Picasso's self-portraits or in the biographies written about him. But there is abundant evidence of powerful and abiding connections to the archetypal unconscious, not the least of which is Picasso's enduring creativity and vitality deep into old age.

Picasso's Minotaur pictures can, I believe, be read as the emergence of his adult imago. His most concentrated expression of the Minotaur image came about in 1933–34, when he was in his early fifties, in the etchings that are contained in the Vollard Suite. At this time, he was ending his marriage with Olga Khokhlova and just recently had fallen in love with the voluptuous young Marie-Thérèse Walter, with whom he soon would have a child. The Minotaur image remained a special personal reference for the remainder of his life. It combines the spiritual nature of the artist and the bestial nature of the physical man—ideal and shadow. It is for Picasso an image of *unio oppositorum,* a god-image as well as a self-image, and it functions in his personality and in his life as an imago. This internal self-definition guided him throughout his remaining years and allowed him the freedom to have and to express his psychic wholeness.

One final image. Picasso painted three explicit self-portraits in the year he died, one of which has been called by many an icon for the twentieth century. Like *Guernica,* this painting is a powerful symbolic statement about the human condition in a time of extreme anguish. The image shows a large ragged face set directly atop a pair of naked shoulders. It depicts, by his own account, Picasso's fear of death. Like his mask paintings, it is *apotropaic,* an attempt to exorcise the fear of the unknown, to diminish the power of "the enemy," in this case

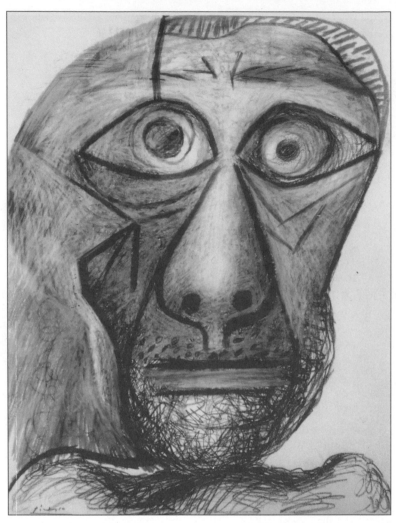

Picasso, Self-Portrait, *1972. Courtesy Fuji Television Gallery.*

identified as death. In the image, the eyes are dominant—wide open, filled with terror, the pupil of the right eye dilated and shot through with blood. The sharp lines around the eyes also speak of chronic fear, and the mouth is clenched shut as though to choke back a scream. It is a face inhuman, or nearly so, resembling that of an ape, perhaps, or a monkey (another of Picasso's favorite self-representations).

Yet it also is human, the visage of a man staring starkly ahead into the menacing maw of death.

Picasso joked with a friend that this painting was his way of exorcising his fear of death,[16] and yet one wonders how effective the exorcism was. To me, this mask speaks of meeting death head on, without the consolation of religion or the comfort of family and friends— nakedly, individually, consciously. In this final image, Picasso shows himself as essentially human, stripped of illusions and the dignity they would bestow. Rembrandt also reached this place of brutal honesty with himself and his onlookers—an old man, bloated, wrinkled, and gray—but his containment in religious iconography held him back from the stark prospect of annihilation and destruction depicted in Picasso's last self-portraits. This has become a symbol for twentieth-century people because so many have had to face their personal mortality without faith in God or a personal afterlife, immediately and without hope marching to war and going into gas chambers and ovens. This has been a century of unrelenting deconstruction and analysis, and Picasso gives us an image that portrays the end station on this cultural path. It is the imago of a man undressed and devoid of illusion, facing the end of life in a state of panic. It is a picture of sheer animal terror. But it is also a mask, and perhaps it has some power to exorcise the demon of death. In Picasso, the imago's link with the animal side of his nature led logically and inexorably to the animal's instinctive reluctance to die.

It is possible that a study of imagos would help to explain biographies by illuminating an important psychological line of development in adulthood. It must, however, be considered as analysis at a relatively abstract macro (not micro) level of detail. It helps to make sense of the details if one can discern the general pattern into which they fit. The imago speaks of the inner terrain of a person's life and indicates the broadest possible boundaries of the pattern that libido assumes in the second half of life. It is a psychic formation that appears during middle adulthood and functions to orient, define, and direct psychic energy. The imago is a living, evolving psychic structure with roots in the archetypal unconscious and ultimately in the self. It both frees people to be what they most deeply are, and it defines who and what they are and what their lives are about. We should be careful not to consider the imago too narrowly, as fixed and defined. Various images approximate it, but none captures it with absolute precision. The sum total of these images may point most clearly to the nature and contours of the underlying psychic structure. Once we grasp a person's imago, we understand something essential about them. We see them whole.

Already, in chapter 2, I have alluded to Jung's adult imago formation as he described it happening in his active imagination experience with the transformative image of Aion. Jung's life has not been read as iconic of modernism in the way Picasso's has, and yet it deeply has touched many modern people who are searching for soul and for a solution to the dilemmas posed by modernity. Despite the Swiss regularity and predictability in his everyday existence, Jung was subjected to the same spiritual and psychological forces of modernity that influenced Picasso, insofar as these were generated in Europe by a general cultural abandonment of religious belief, by loss of faith in Western values and the idea of progress so central to them, and by the urgent need to find adequate images to express full selfhood outside the confines of traditional religious culture. Jung was a thoroughly modern man, but we must note that, while he lived his adult life in the same century as Picasso, his cultural context was Protestant Middle Europe. More precisely, his lifelong containment in bourgeois Swiss family life and in the established profession of medicine gives his biography a tone much different from Picasso's life, with its Spanish background, Parisian flavor, and unfettered bohemianism. Both men felt the necessity to burst the bonds of tradition—indeed, to challenge and transform it. In Picasso's case, it was the artistic tradition that needed to be challenged; in Jung's case, it was scientific and religious traditions. Jung did not depict his various moltings and major transformations in self-portraits on canvas as Rembrandt and Picasso did. Rather, they can be traced, for the most part, in written accounts of his inner experiences—dreams, active imagination, fantasy images—and, most importantly for this chapter, in an architectural statement that I shall consider as a final portrait of his imago, the stone tower at Bollingen.

Of the three lives considered in this chapter, Jung's was the one most self-consciously aimed at, and articulated as, psychological transformation. Rembrandt left nothing in writing to indicate his state of self-awareness, and Picasso shunned psychological interpretation and verbal self-disclosure. Of these three figures, Jung alone offered an explicit account of his psychological process and a personal statement of its meaning. His own life became a kind of psychological laboratory for him, and he carefully observed and recorded what unfolded there.

As a transforming person, Jung shows some of the same traits in his relation to psychology that Rembrandt and Picasso demonstrate in their relation to art. All three figures took up their chosen professions in an established context that contained exemplars, models of career building, methods of proceeding with the task at hand; and all three transformed these given models and patterns into a unique expression of their own. One could describe them all as rebels who, once they thoroughly had mastered their craft, used their enormous individual talent to defy the collective rules and go it alone. But this would describe adequately only the first half of their lives, the caterpillar stage. The adult imago, which follows a vigorously expansive youth, defines the personality's essence and indicates a person's capacity for wholeness. In the cases we are studying here, the adult imago emerges only after the way has been cleared for a novel and relatively unrestrained individual development. As neither Rembrandt nor Picasso could paint happily on commission and follow the career path usual for artists in their time, so Jung broke the mold of psychiatrist and psychoanalyst, resigned his academic position as professor of psychiatry, and sought his own way of being a modern psychologist. Rembrandt eventually assumed the imago of archetypal artist combined with the spiritual enlightenment of a Saint Paul. Picasso found in the Minotaur image the combination of opposites that allowed him full expression of his adult being, within the boundaries of a classical imago; eventually he assumed the mask of a death-haunted modern Everyman. What, then, was Jung's destiny, his final imago?

It is noteworthy that all three of these figures reached back to ancient classical images to define themselves. Classical images carry the charge of the archetypal psyche. Chapter 2 discusses Jung's report of turning into the mythic figure Aion during an active imagination in 1913. This had been preceded immediately by an image of crucifixion, in which Jung was identified with Christ, and it led to the healing of his anima Salome's blindness. This is Jung's most dramatic account on record of deification, of actual union with archetypal images and energies. Occurring in Jung's thirty-ninth year, this extraordinary occasion signaled the onset of his midlife transformation. The ensuing metamorphosis would change his identity and set him off in directions that could not have been foretold so clearly in his larval stage. Naturally the imaginal disks were there from the beginning and can be discerned throughout his biography, but the fully formed imago did not emerge until 1928, when Jung was fifty-three. This imago would allow Jung to transcend his times and his cultural conditioning, and assume his place as one of the great healers of soul and spiritual teachers of the age.

A careful student of rhetoric will note a change in tone in Jung's writings after 1928. His early writings begin in 1900, with the publication of his doctoral dissertation on so-called mediumistic phenomena. They go on to include the book on dementia praecox (schizophrenia), the studies in word association, many papers on psychiatric topics, contributions to Freudian thought, and, in 1912, the culminating work of the early period, *Wandlungen und Symbole der Libido*. Except for the last, these are purely rational, academic, scientific works. *Wandlungen* verges on the visionary and is a bit overwrought, disorganized, and extravagant in its claims and hypotheses; nevertheless, it is a work of remarkable intellectual power, a *tour de force*. Then there follows an era of relative silence during the years of midlife crisis and World War I, a silence broken in 1921 by publication of the massive, somewhat pedantic work, *Psychological Types*, a summary of work to date and a major contribution to the study of character formation and psychodynamics. A sharp rhetorical shift becomes apparent in 1928, with the publication of his "Commentary on *The Secret of the Golden Flower.*" In this work, published in conjunction with Richard Wilhelm's translation of a Chinese masterpiece, Jung for the first time takes on the rhetorical mantle of the spiritual teacher, and his writing never will be quite the same again. At fifty-three, he has found his mature voice, which in the following years will become recognized universally as the voice of a spiritual master. At times he will play it down before a specific audience, but this voice is what will draw students from all over the world to study with him, the sage of Küsnacht.

We can study the period of transformation in Jung's life with some precision because he offers a lot of detail about it in his autobiography. As described there, the period of pupation fell into two major phases. The first phase (1912–16) consisted of opening up to the unconscious psyche with all of its frightful, teeming variety and symbolic richness; Jung was flooded with psychic material and nearly overwhelmed. The second phase (1916–28) was calmer and was characterized by a centering process, which appeared first as a series of mandala images and then culminated in 1928 in a dream (the "Liverpool dream"[17]) which conveyed to him a fully convincing image of the self. For Jung, this landmark dream's message was that he had gone as far as he would go in plumbing the depths of the psyche. He had found the irreducible center. And so he arrived at his defining myth, conceptualized as the self. Articulating this myth and living out its implications would occupy him for the remainder of his long life (he died at the age of eighty-six). The image and the concept of the self most centrally defined the adult Jung and constituted his adult imago. From this imago and the perspective on psychological reality it offered, Jung created his later contributions to analytical psychology.

The self became the dominant theme in Jung's writings after 1928. It is importantly featured in the alchemical writings, which date from 1928 to 1955 and the publication of *Mysterium Coniunctionis;* but it is most explicitly and systematically expounded in the work, *Aion,* published in 1951. In *Aion,* Jung once again picked up the image of this mythic figure whom he personally had experienced so vividly in

1913, and in this late text he employed it to establish a vantage point outside of time, as it were, from which to look at Western cultural history and the Christian era. Recall that the myth of Aion locates Jung beyond the rule of time—he actually is the ruler over time. Then we can observe how Jung used this association with the transcendent principle behind astrological time to reflect upon the inner history and meaning of Christianity up to the present time in the Age of Pisces. He goes on to speculate about the Platonic Year to come, the Age of Aquarius. At the heart of this work's agenda, however, lies the attempt to offer an account of the structure and dynamics of the self as an archetypal factor that, like *Aion*, exists outside the ego's world of time-space categories. This factor shapes the psychological structures and unfolding developments of individuals, as well as the Zeitgeist of whole epochs. *Aion* is a work that attempts to see the personal and the collective historical dimensions of life as united in a meaningful set of rhythms and deployments in time.

One thing which neither Rembrandt nor Picasso, who were equally transforming persons, tried to do explicitly and self-consciously, but which Jung did attempt, was to dream the collective religious myth onward, to take it beyond its present state of decrepitude through a transformation process into a new era of its internal development.[18] Rembrandt accepted it as given; Picasso lived the myth of the modern man. Jung tried to go one step farther. Perhaps the heroic side of Jung expressed itself in this undertaking; certainly this latter also was an attempt to complete his father's unfinished business with Christian faith. For, through books, letters, and lectures, he actually engaged the (to him) nearly defunct Biblical tradition in an interactive dialogical process that is based in a Rebis structure grown up between them. He offers the West a new religious symbol—the Quaternity— to attract energy and to carry its collective libido forward in time and in internal development toward completion and wholeness. This effort to transform the central religious image of Christianity—its image of God as a Trinity—is passionately inscribed in his book *Answer to Job*, arguably Jung's most controversial published work and one that cost him several important relationships with Christian clergy (not least, that of the highly regarded Benedictine priest, Vic-

Jung's tower at Bollingen. Photograph by Ruth Ammann.

tor White). This text has been seen by some commentators as the basis of a new doctrinal development in Western religion[19] and by others as a statement of Jung's inflation.[20] In any event, it was an attempt on his part to generate a transformative dynamic within Christian theology and culture. A central thrust of it is the rising star of the feminine within an ancient patriarchal tradition. Jung saw a deep need for integration in what has been a highly divisive—even "splitting"—spiritual tradition.

Besides expounding the self in his writings and psychological teaching, however, Jung also represented it in concrete material form in his one and only architectural undertaking, the stone tower at Bollingen. In 1922 he bought the land for it, a piece of property at the upper end of Lake Zurich. He carefully notes that the place "formerly belonged to the monastery of St. Gall."[21] It would become his own personal hermitage, "a confession of faith in stone."[22] Over the course of the following twelve years, in four phases, each separated by four years (1923, 1927, 1931, 1935), a structure was built of locally hewn granite. Jung considered it a representation of the self. For our purposes, we can consider it a self-portrait of Jung's imago, an expression of his fully realized adult form.

The first part of the tower initially was conceived as a simple African hut (note the fascination with things African, held in common by Jung and Picasso). It was intended to concretize "an idea of wholeness, a familial wholeness in which all sorts of small domestic animals likewise participate."[23] This part of the tower would cling to the earth and embrace the body and the instincts. Jung here was grounding his imago in physical existence, again not unlike Picasso's elemental relation to body and instinct, as represented in the Minotaur. For Jung, the self was rooted in flesh and blood, in the body. He soon decided on a more European two-story structure, but to him the structure still represented "the maternal hearth."[24] He began his architectural statement by putting in place the deep preoedipal psychic structures and building up from there.

In 1927, he erected a towerlike annex which became the central feature of the building, now a "tower." The spirit had begun to arise from the maternal ground, and the phallic masculine next appeared. This annex was extended in 1931 to include a private room where he could be utterly alone, a space of interiority and retreat, upon whose walls he painted the image of his inner teacher, Philemon, the winged bald sage who, he says, taught him how to become objective about the psyche.[25] This came to be "a place of spiritual concentration,"[26] where he could enter the realm of timeless archetypal images, a doorway to the eternal spirit. Thus, body and spirit—maternal hearth and kitchen, tower and meditation center—were joined in the emergent structure. For Jung, this is the most fundamental polarity in the self.

Finally, in 1935, he completed the building with a courtyard and loggia by the lake, which connected the building to its surroundings, especially the lake, and offered Jung the opportunity to carve and display his imaginal inner world in stone. The tower now looked outward to its surroundings and assumed a place in relationship to the immediate landscape. The building remained in this form until 1955, when, after the death of his wife, Jung added a story to the small central section. This, he says, represented his ego-personality, the "extension of consciousness achieved in old age."[27] It was an extension upward. This same "extension" is what we find in Rembrandt's late self-portraits and also, though in a distinctly "modern" form, in Picasso's last self-portraits. In its final form, the Bollingen tower represents the complete expression of Jung's imago as it was constituted after midlife and realized in the second half of life. It is a statement in stone of psychological wholeness, which represents the full emergence of the self in Jung's adulthood and embraces the physical and spiritual dimensions of life. In a sense, Jung's imago embraces both the spirituality of Rembrandt's late statement in his self-portrait as the Apostle Paul and the physicality of Picasso's final image, uniting them into a single whole.

There is a strong stylistic flavor of European medievalism and Christian traditionalism in the Bollingen tower, yet it also self-consciously bespeaks the twentieth century. Of its time, it also transcends it. It contains a mixture of styles—primitive, pagan, and classical, as well as medieval—that mark it as post-Christian in its self-awareness. This combination of "quotations" could be read as an anticipation of the vocabulary of postmodernism. But Jung would eschew all such labels and classifications. In his own terms, what he was doing was intuitively groping his way toward a statement of psychological wholeness. He was seeking a combination of elements that would hold his own inner opposites together in a creative tension and would embody an image of wholeness in which even his remote ancestors would feel at home (hence no plumbing or electricity). Like his inner world of dreams and fantasy images, the tower embraces the ages and touches on many polarities: mother-father, material-spiritual, good-evil, ancient-modern, traditional-exotic, male-female. It is a testament in stone to his psychic imago.

In preparation for death, Jung found an attitude, created from his "imaginal disks"—as they arrived in dreams and active imagination—that would carry him forward, if not with the brave assurance of a Rembrandt, nevertheless confidently, with the measured grace of a flower falling to earth and reconnecting with its original underground rhizome.[28] What he achieved in life was the realization of an archetypal imago that contains both spiritual wisdom and earthy grounding. He lived a full human life and became a sage, a teacher for his age and for ages to come. Like Rembrandt and Picasso, Jung himself was transformed by the ageless images of the collective unconscious. In turn, he sought to place his grain of sand on the scales of history and so move the eternal spirit one more tick in the direction of full incarnation.

Epilogue

She is dreaming again.

She has been given a special telephone number. With it come three blue stones shot through with gold, which must be used to gain access to the telephone line. Someone informs her that the number has become available at this time because the person who had it previously is not being offered a renewal. That person is angry, but there is only a limited quantity of these numbers. For some reason that person was not reelected. She realizes that these stones cannot be used in regular public telephones, and at first she is inclined to pass up the offer. But the stones are beautiful and pleasant to hold and to rub together in her pocket, so she decides to keep them. Suddenly she finds herself in a place where some Native American "holy people" are working on advanced transformations. They work in small groups in an enclosed space, like a kiva, and call forth transformations in one another. They are very quiet and focused. Somehow she receives a message that there are people here— visitors, tourists, and some other Native Americans as well— who do not belong at this ceremony, who should not witness this or try to reach this depth too quickly. They are in earlier stages and will not understand what is going on. It might even harm them. She is instructed to distract these people by performing a low-level transformation to take attention away from the holy people. So she performs the simplest transformation, which is to levitate a few feet above the ground, and she floats around the room. In this way, she captures their attention and holds it while the deep transformations take place. The dream ends here.

It is apparent in our time that Western culture, and indeed all world cultures, are going through a dark phase of internal transformation. Perhaps, at the same time, there are spiritually advanced individuals who are pushing ahead to new spiritual frontiers. What we see more evidently is that old religions and social structures are breaking down, patterns of community and family life are disintegrating, and compensatory efforts are being made to shore up the certainties of the past by regressing to one of the many fundamentalisms among the world's religions. Notions such as "It takes a whole village to raise a child" meet with little response when there are no longer any villages.[1] To say that our cities are jungles is to insult nature. They are in many respects war zones fought over by rival gangs of adolescent and post-adolescent males. Nearly half the babies in the United States today are born out of wedlock, and one-fourth of the children live below the poverty line. Beyond that, we suffer from a youth culture without the *joie de vivre* that is supposed to emanate from the young, for in truth we are a dying civilization on its last legs.

I look upon this as pupation and refuse to think that the archetypes have abandoned us. We are in a social and cultural regression, and the imaginal disks that will shape the future are taking form and will emerge. The new imago has not yet appeared; it is unknown and invisible culturally, religiously, and socially—that is, collectively. Yet one can have faith that it is growing in the silent depths of the world's collective unconscious and will, in its own time, in a moment of *kairos,* make its appearance. Meanwhile, we live in an era of analysis and deconstruction, when the images and symbols that have been perceived as substantial and undergirding are being rendered useless and shown to be hollow and meaningless constructions. Not only have the dogmas and creeds of traditional religions been declared vain mythological confabulations of social and political interest groups, but the very ideologies and intellectual movements that have deconstructed those edifices have been deconstructed themselves or are being so even as we speak. Peel the onion far enough, and one finds there is no core. The modern mandala is empty at its center, Jung noted exactly sixty years ago in his Terry Lectures at Yale University. The decades since then have confirmed this observation, and today we are closer than ever to a nihilistic consensus. Picasso's late self-portrait is a defining image for this age. The poet Auden called this an age of anxiety. We can add that it is an age of emptiness.

The violence that surrounds us and eats away at urban culture internally is a byproduct of this nihilistic spirit. Its ubiquity cannot be diminished by mechanically stemming the flow of drugs, adding jobs in inner cities, or building more fast-food joints and multiplex cinemas to distract, feed, and entertain the restless. Our violence is not primary but rather derives from the absence of defining images that would harness the energy of the psyche and give it a meaningful, constructive expression. It is such transforming images that one must await as we move anxiously forward in the dark night of this collective soul.

The question becomes, then, where to look for images of transformation. From what quarter will they emerge? Where can we expect an annunciation? If past experience is a guide, the revelation comes unexpectedly to the individual in a moment of vision, a surprise gift from the unconscious. A voice speaks from a burning bush, an angel appears to a virgin, Rilke hears a line of poetry in the wind, Jung drops into an abyss and experiences deification. From such transformative images an inner psychological process of pupation—quiet pregnancy—is engendered. A period of internal deconstruction and rearrangement of structural elements, sometimes in solitude and sometimes in the alchemy of intimate union with another, arrives at its goal of creating the imago, the Rebis, the image that gathers energy about it and directs it into channels of meaningful effort. From this central imago the individual acts and thereby becomes a transformational figure for others. Rilke transforms poetry, Picasso painting, Jung psychoanalysis. These figures have become reference points for late twentieth-century culture in the West—indeed, increasingly, worldwide. The source of their contributions in each case was the archetypal world of images individually experienced and appropriated in a unique way. Each personally was transformed by the archetypal image and, having pupated, then lived and worked from a center of energy, transforming his context as a result.

One could cite many more examples of such transforming persons, historical and contemporary. Famous and anonymous individuals have gone through personal experiences of transformation and, having found their centers in a defining image, consequently have channeled their energies into activities and lives of creativity and meaning. No longer looking to collective structures to contain them or to provide access to transformation, modern (and now postmodern) individuals look to their own immediate experience of transformative images and relationships for guidance and resource. The arrivals of annunciation, deification, transformation have been democratized. No longer something that happened once upon a time for all of humankind, the annunciation comes to you and me, here and now, personally, in a dream, an active imagination, a synchronistic event, an I-Thou relationship of profound union between two people. The contemporary attitude therefore is at once more and less modest than the traditional one. Transformation in the sublime sense of deification now is universally available. The models of the past, idealized as demigods and superhuman heroes, have been deconstructed, demythologized, and rendered merely historical— human, all too human. This has released the individual from the bondage of idolatry and opened the way for the transformation of many.

The distinction, made in the dream above, among stages or levels of transformation, and among people who do or do not achieve them, speaks also of a kind of spiritual elite, however. At the ego and persona level—the collective, its rules and laws—we citizens of the Western democracies easily can agree that all people ought to be treated as equals. But as soon as movement, development, strivings for achievement and excellence are introduced, there is a rapid separation into layers and levels, based on potential and effort. Not everyone can be Michael Jordan on the basketball court; and, as Michael Jordan learned, not even he can be Mickey Mantle on the baseball diamond. Child prodigies have performed difficult violin concertos at the age of five or six. In all areas of human activity there are exceptional geniuses, average achievers, and slow learners. It is the same in matters psychological and spiritual. While everyone who works at it can achieve imago status as an adult human being to some degree and become all they are created to be as a person, not all can go as far in the "advanced transformations" indicated by the dream. For the imago is not only an image created in the eyes of the world at the level of ego and persona, but much more it is inner development that takes the ego out of its world and into the archetypal realm of the spirit and the self. At these levels, some people have a degree of ability and openness that is exceptional. Their lives show an extraordinary degree of uniqueness, imagination, and pristine individuality. They are leaders in the area of spiritual direction. Perhaps they can show a way through the dark times to come.

Experience with the archetypal transformative images creates an attitude in people that breaks through every kind of narrow provincialism. This is an elect that does not set itself apart from others on account of tribal, racial, ethnic, or traditional religious stripes and markings. While defining the individual as unique, it also states the individual's identity in universal terms. The person becomes a man for all times, a woman of the world. Kinship is extended to humanity as such, personal awareness opens to global perspectives and to ecological sensitivity worldwide. A new tension of opposites then emerges, one which combines the uniqueness of the individual with the collective nature of the transformative image on which identity is based. The unique and the universal become united in the individually human.

Can this vision of wholeness be communicated on worldwide television, in cyberspace on the Internet, in popular music and advertising? Can it become planetary? The media, which today are homogenizing the world's cultures, may be useful or may constitute obstacles. The collective values that are communicated by blue jeans, McDonald's outlets, Walt Disney movies, and Coca-Cola advertisements may be the harbingers of emergent world culture or germs of further decay and disintegration. Futurologists play games, modeling strategies and statistical analyses. Most often they cannot foresee what is ahead. As we rush forward, transformations of all sorts are sure to materialize, surprising us in their novelty and frightening us in their unfamiliarity. A few will command wide collective attention and gather energy around their emergent centers. The individual who is not grounded in a personal experience of transformation will be swept easily into the vortex of collective transforming images and energies. The question becomes acute: are variety, diversity, and psychological uniqueness to prevail, or will collective uniformity, homogeneity, and sameness push aside the individual?

A woman dreams of a small group of Native Americans performing advanced transformations. Observers and tourists, who are of a different spiritual order, need to be distracted until they too are ready to partake in the full ritual. To me, it seems crucial to discover on which side of this division one lives, for between transformation and entertainment lies a great divide. The deeper transformations always have been reserved for a small minority, and I am sure this will not change greatly, even in the twenty-first century, the Age of Aquarius, and whatever lies beyond the horizon of our knowing.

NOTES

Foreword

1. D. H. Rosen, *Transforming Depression: Healing the Soul Through Creativity* (New York: Penguin, 1996).
2. C. G. Jung, "Basic Postulates of Analytical Psychology," in *The Structure and Dynamics of the Psyche,* in *The Collected Works of C. G. Jung* (Princeton, N.J.: Princeton Univ. Press, 1978), 8:357.
3. W. James, *The Varieties of Religious Experience: A Study in Human Nature* (New York: Longmans, Green, 1912), 228–30.
4. Ibid., 166.
5. C. G. Jung, "Picasso," in *The Spirit in Man, Art, and Literature,* in *The Collected Works of C. G. Jung* (Princeton, N.J.: Princeton Univ. Press, 1966), 15:135–41.
6. M. Buber, *Good and Evil* (New York: Charles Scribner's Sons, 1953), 5.

Chapter 1

Epigraph from C. G. Jung, *Two Essays in Analytical Psychology,* in *The Collected Works of C. G. Jung* (Princeton, N.J.: Princeton Univ. Press, 1966), 7:291.

1. This dream is reprinted from Murray Stein, *In MidLife* (Dallas, Tex.: Spring Publications, 1983), 126–28, and is quoted here because it is such an impressive example, in a modern psyche's individual rendition, of the ancient and ubiquitous analogy between human transformation and the metamorphosis of the butterfly. This dream is based on a widely used, perhaps even universal, metaphor.
2. In contrasting his position with Freud's, Jung used the metaphor of cater-

pillar-to-butterfly transformation. He said that a person lives in a caterpillar stage, which is pre-sexual, until adolescence, at which point he or she metamorphoses into a fully sexual being, the "butterfly" (C. G. Jung, *Collected Works* [New York: Pantheon, Bollingen Series, 1961] 4:104–19). In this work I use the same metaphor to speak about the emergence of the self in the second half of life. To be consistent with Jung's schema, we could say there are two major metamorphoses in the life cycle: the first in adolescence, when we become fully sexual; the second in adulthood, when the self unfolds fully.

3. See Erik Erikson, *The Life Cycle Completed: A Review* (New York: Norton, 1982), on the eight stages of development. This plan is not incompatible with Jung's developmental schema for the life cycle. In fact, Erikson adds detail where Jung is not very specific, especially on pre-adolescent phases of growth.

4. George Lakoff and Mark Johnson, *Metaphors We Live By* (Chicago: Univ. of Chicago Press, 1980), 3. It is noteworthy that Jung opens his *Wandlungen und Symbole der Libido* (Leipzig and Vienna: Franz Deuticke, 1912) with a distinction between two types of thinking: directed thinking and metaphorical or imagistic thinking. The latter often underlies, precedes, or extends the former.

5. David Rosen, *Transforming Depression,* presents the most up-to-date and complete Jungian approach to the treatment of depression. Generally Jungian analysts see depression as an essential part of the transformation process. Unless it is a major depression and debilitating, or instigated by somatic rather than psychological causes, they treat it in psychotherapy.

6. This also has been called the Peter Pan Syndrome. It is development arrested in the adolescent phase. The classic Jungian study of this is Marie-Louise von Franz, *Puer Aeternus: A Psychological Study of the Adult Struggle with the Paradise of Childhood,* 2d ed. (Santa Monica, Calif.: Sigo Press, 1981).

7. Adolf Portmann, "Metamorphosis in Animals: The Transformations of the Individual and the Type," in *Man and Transformation,* ed. Joseph Campbell (New York: Bollingen Foundation, 1964), 299.

8. Ibid.

9. Jung was amazed at the profundity and prescience of "the dreams of three- and four-year-old children, among which there are some so strikingly mythological and so fraught with meaning that one would take them at

once for the dreams of grown-ups . . . They are the last vestiges of a dwin-
dling collective psyche which dreamingly reiterates the perennial contents
of the human soul." C. G. Jung, *The Collected Works of C. G. Jung,*
(Princeton, N.J.: Princeton Univ. Press, 1964), 17:94.

10. Jean Chevalier and Alain Gheerbrant, *A Dictionary of Symbols* (Oxford,
England: Blackwell Publisher, 1994), 140–41.

11. Portmann, "Metamorphosis," 301.

12. Ibid.

13. Alexander B. Klots, *The World of Butterflies and Moths* (New York:
McGraw-Hill, 1950), 44.

14. C. A. Meier, *Healing Dream and Ritual: Ancient Incubation and Modern Psychotherapy* (Evanston, Ill.: Northwestern Univ. Press, 1967), relates this
theme to the healing rites in the Asclepian temples of ancient Greece.

15. Portmann, "Metamorphosis," 299–300.

16. Klots, *World of Butterflies,* 35.

17. Portmann, "Metamorphosis," 306.

18. Wolfgang Leppmann, *Rilke: A Life* (New York: Fromm International, 1984), 3.

19. Stephen Mitchell, ed., *The Selected Poetry of Rainer Maria Rilke,* trans. Stephen Mitchell (New York: Random House, 1982), 315. This is a quotation
from Princess Marie von Thurn und Taxis-Hohenlohe, *Erinnerungen an
Rainer Maria Rilke,* 40.

20. Mitchell translation, from *Selected Poetry,* 151. Unless otherwise indicated,
all translated material from the *Elegies* is from Rainer Maria Rilke, *Duino
Elegies,* trans. David Oswald (Einsiedeln, Switzerland: Daimon Verlag, 1992).

21. Translation of this line is by Ruth Ilg, private communication.

22. I thank Ruth Ilg for helping me get this sequence correct.

23. Donald Prater, *A Ringing Glass: The Life of Rainer Maria Rilke* (Oxford,
England: Clarendon Press, 1986), 207.

24. Ibid., 324.

25. "René, which stems from the Roman name Renatur, was originally a man's
name—only over time did it become a woman's name in France with the
different spelling, but same pronunciation. Rainer also spelled Reiner, has
always been a man's name—it stems from *Reginher: ragin* = advice, decision; and *hari* = army, troop." Ruth Ilg, personal communication.

26. Rainer Maria Rilke, *Duino Elegies and The Sonnets to Orpheus,* translated
by A. Poulin, Jr. Boston: Houghton Mifflin, 1977.

27. C. G. Jung, *The Collected Works of C. G. Jung* (Princeton, N.J.: Princeton Univ. Press, 1969), 11:338.

Chapter 2

Epigraph from Jung, *Two Essays,* 7:233.

1. Glenn Fowler, "W. L. Mellon, Humanitarian, Is Dead at 79," *New York Times,* Feb. 24, 1991, p. 15.
2. William McGuire, *The Freud-Jung Letters* (Princeton, N.J.: Princeton Univ. Press, 1974), 487.
3. C. G. Jung, *Analytical Psychology: Notes to the Seminar Held 1925* (Princeton, N.J.: Princeton Univ. Press, 1989), 92–99.
4. Ibid., 96.
5. Ibid., 99.
6. Ibid., 98.
7. F. M. Cornford, *The Unwritten Philosophy and Other Essays* (Cambridge, England: Cambridge Univ. Press, 1950), 77.
8. Jung, *Analytical Psychology,* 98.
9. Ibid., 97.
10. C. G. Jung, *Memories, Dreams, Reflections,* recorded and edited by Aniela Jaffé (New York: Vintage Books, 1961) 182.
11. C. G. Jung, *Symbols of Transformation,* in *The Collected Works of C. G. Jung* (Princeton, N.J.: Princeton Univ. Press, 1967), 5:223.
12. *Shorter Oxford English Dictionary* (Oxford, England: Clarendon Press, 1973), 2344.
13. McGuire, *Freud-Jung Letters.*
14. Cornford, *Unwritten Philosophy,* 77.
15. Murray Stein, *Jung's Treatment of Christianity* (Wilmette, Ill.: Chiron Publications, 1985), ch. 4.

Chapter 3

Epigraph from C. G. Jung, "The Psychology of the Transference," in *The Practice of Psychotherapy,* in *The Collected Works of C. G. Jung* (Princeton, N.J.: Princeton Univ. Press, 1966), 16:454.

1. If it is a question of repression, the process is different. It then becomes a matter of righting an old wrong. For example, feeling types sometimes are cowed into conforming to thinking type standards and expectations in school, and it is a matter of recovery for them to take back their true superior function in adulthood. People who have been homosexually inclined throughout life but afraid to live their preferences also will experience the acceptance of their gender preference as a process of transformation in adulthood. What I am speaking of in this book is different, however. It normally has to do not with recovering repressed aspects of the self but with realizing potentials that have been dormant until the timing was right for them to appear.

2. I owe this suggestion to David Rosen, private communication.

3. For detailed documentation of the relationship between Jung and Spielrein, see John Kerr, *A Most Dangerous Method: The Story of Jung, Freud, and Sabina Spielrein* (New York: Knopf, 1993). Kerr goes into all of the available material and writes in a style that is easily accessible to the general reader. It is a fascinating study of mutual influences, many of them unknown until recently.

4. McGuire, *Freud-Jung Letters*, 7.

5. Ibid., 93.

6. Merton Gill, *Psychoanalysis in Transition* (Hillsdale, N.J.: Analytic Press, 1994), 33–47. Gill offers a critique of the "one person situation" and proposes a model that is somewhat more in line with Jung's conception of an interactive matrix in analysis. In distinguishing psychoanalysis from psychotherapy, however, he still holds out for the centrality of transference analysis: "The decisive criterion of psychoanalysis . . . is that transference—the patient's experience of the interaction—is analyzed as much as is possible, whereas in psychotherapy it is to a greater or lesser degree willingly left unanalyzed" (62).

7. Aldo Carotenuto, *Secret Symmetry: Sabina Spielrein Between Freud and Jung* (New York: Pantheon, 1982; rev. ed., 1983). The English version of this book contains only Spielrein's letters to Jung. The German version, *Tagebuch einer heimlichen Symmetric: Sabina Spielrein zwischen Jung und Freud* (Freiburg im Breisgau, Germany: Kore, 1986), includes Jung's side of the correspondence.

8. C. G. Jung, "Problems of Modern Psychotherapy," in *The Practice of Psycho-therapy,* in *The Collected Works of C. G. Jung* (Princeton, N.J.: Princeton Univ. Press, 1966), 16:124.

9. Ibid., 16:139.

10. In a letter to Freud dated Oct. 28, 1907, Jung confesses: "Actually—and I confess this to you with a struggle—I have a boundless admiration for you both as a man and a researcher . . . my veneration for you has something of the character of a 'religious' crush. Though it does not really bother me, I still feel it is disgusting and ridiculous because of its undeniable erotic undertone. This abominable feeling comes from the fact that as a boy I was the victim of a sexual assault by a man I once worshipped" (McGuire, *Freud-Jung Letters,* 95). Details of this incident of sexual abuse in Jung's childhood have not yet come to light.

11. Jung, "Problems of Modern Psychotherapy," 16:145.

12. Ibid., 16:163.

13. Michael Fordham, "Countertransference," in *Explorations into the Self,* by Michael Fordham (London: Academic Press, 1985), 142–43.

14. Ibid., 143, refers to this as the "syntonic" countertransference.

15. Jung, "Psychology of Transference," 16:431.

16. Ibid., 16:368.

17. Ibid., 16:407.

18. The discussion of the "transformational object," in Christopher Bollas, *The Shadow of the Object* (New York: Columbia Univ. Press, 1987), 13–29, locates it in a regression to the maternal level of object relations. He follows Winnicott in thinking of it as a transitional object. Since he does not utilize the theory of archetypes, he fails to find the full dimensions of this object. Actually it is an archetypal object that appears as a symbol of transformation during deep regression. Jessica Benjamin, *Like Subjects, Love Objects* (New Haven, Conn.: Yale Univ. Press, 1995), 145 n3, comes closer to this view in following Michael Eigen, who is knowledgeable about Jung and archetypal theory, and in then speaking about the creation of symbols and the stimulation of imagination in regression.

19. Jung, "Psychology of Transference," 16:476.

20. Following Bion, Fordham, in "Countertransference," 143, suggests that the analyst try "divesting himself of memory and desire. These would be

expressing themselves as preconceptions about the therapy and the patient and not knowing what could or what ought to be done or thought."

21. Jung, "Commentary on *The Secret of the Golden Flower*," in *Alchemical Studies*, in *The Collected Works of C. G. Jung* (Princeton, N.J.: Princeton Univ. Press, 1967), 13:20, comments on the attitude of *wu wei*: "The art of letting things happen, action through non-action, letting go of oneself as taught by Meister Eckhart, became for me the key that opens the door to the Way. We must be able to let things happen in the psyche."

22. Fordham, "Countertransference," 144.

23. Jung, "Psychology of Transference," 16:537.

24. Jung, *Analytical Psychology*, 99.

25. Jung, "Psychology of Transference," 16:531.

26. Jung, *Memories, Dreams, Reflections*, 315.

27. Ibid., 296.

28. C. G. Jung, "Marriage as a Psychological Relationship," in *The Development of Personality*, in *The Collected Works of C. G. Jung* (Princeton, N.J.: Princeton Univ. Press, 1964), 17:332ff.

Chapter 4

Epigraph from Jung, *Two Essays*, 7:404.

1. In a famous BBC interview with John Freeman, Jung was asked if he believed in God. His reply, "I do not believe, I know," drew many questions and comments. In that interview, Jung went on to say that he never could "believe" anything solely on the basis of traditional authority and teaching; rather, he had a scientific mind and needed to know things on the basis of facts and evidence. He implies that he knows about God through personal experience. This kind of "knowing," however, is personal and "gnostic," not scientifically verifiable or disconfirmable. William McGuire and R. F. C. Hull, eds., *C. G. Jung Speaking* (Princeton, N.J.: Princeton Univ. Press, 1977), 428.

2. It is not universally the case that people achieve full imagos; not all individuate to the same degree. There are at least two ways to understand this. It can be argued that, given similar lifespans and approximately similar opportunities, individual differences in outcome are due to psychopathol-

ogy. That is, everyone has the opportunity to transform into a full human imago, but the psychopathology generated by trauma and the individual's inherent sensitivities to environmental conditions prevent this full development from taking place. Some people's development becomes arrested at an early stage; while others, who have no more innate potential for development but do have better nurturance and/or tougher skins, achieve full development or at least push it to the maximum extent possible. An alternative view is that some people simply are destined from the outset—by genetics or archetypal constellation—to go farther than others, since they are "old souls" to begin with. It can be argued that human nature is not "even" or "equal" when it comes to developmental potential. Some people are endowed better physically, others psychologically and spiritually. Therefore there are great differences in psychological outcome by virtue of innate differences. The second is the more fatalistic view. Both can claim that they are realistic. I prefer a position that combines these two and holds that there are many different possible human imagos, just as there are many varieties of butterfly. Some of these are judged by cultural standards and moral norms to be deficient and not even to qualify as imagos. In addition, there are many instances of failed development, due to pathologies that are attributable either to innate genetic limitations and lack of proper nurture, in which the process is arrested in the caterpillar or the pupal stage and an imago never appears. This combination of factors, including both nature and nurture viewpoints, accounts most completely, it seems to me, for the wide variety in levels and outcomes of development in adulthood. It remains for further research to determine the relative weight of each of these factors.

The selective nature of spiritual life has been acknowledged by the spiritual traditions in their distinctions between lay and religious members. Some people are called to greater efforts and even to "unnatural" lifestyles in order to gain enlightenment or full spiritual fulfillment.

3. Pascal Bonafoux, *Rembrandt: Master of the Portrait* (New York: Harry N. Abrams, 1990), 109.
4. John Richardson, *A Life of Picasso* (New York: Random House, 1996), 2:9.
5. "Pablo Picasso: Assessment," in *Encyclopedia Britannica*.
6. Ibid.
7. John Richardson, quoted in Kirk Varnedoe, "Picasso's Self-Portraits," in

Picasso and Portraiture: Representation and Transformation, ed. William
Rubin (New York: Museum of Modern Art, 1996), 113.

8. Varnedoe, "Picasso's Self-Portraits," 113.

9. Picasso quoted in Richardson, *Life of Picasso,* 2:24.

10. Ibid., 1:471.

11. Ibid., 2:9.

12. Varnedoe, "Picasso's Self-Portraits," 138.

13. Richardson, *Life of Picasso,* 2:9, on this portrait, says: "Inspiration for this
    portrait (now in the Prague National Gallery) did not come from any of
    Picasso's previous exemplars—El Greco, Cézanne or Gauguin—but from
    Van Gogh and a totally new source: the cinema. The artist was a past mas-
    ter of self-dramatization, and the look of menace on Picasso's face derives,
    at least in part, from the stylized close-ups in the silent movies of which
    the artist was such a fan: close-ups where the eyes, graphically accentuated,
    as here, in black, double for the silent mouth and articulate the hero's sang-
    froid, the villain's glee, the artist's mad resolve. This work is the quintes-
    sence of the Andalusian *mirada fuerte,* the strong gaze, that Picasso turned
    on people he wanted to conquer, seduce, possess, and, not least, shock."

14. Ibid., 2:103.

15. The discovery of this healing image may have saved Picasso's sanity. Clearly
    he had the potential for rather severe psychotic disturbance; witness his
    comments on African masks quoted in the text, his violent relationships
    with women, and the obvious paranoia he exhibited toward the world.
    Jung, in a famous 1932 essay on Picasso published in the *Neue Zürcher Zeit-
    ung,* commented that Picasso's paintings revealed a psyche that, if it were
    to fall into serious mental illness, would become schizophrenic rather than
    neurotic; Jung, "Picasso," in *Collected Works,* 15:135–41. In the African mask
    and Greek mythological images, Picasso found, as he said, a means of exor-
    cising his demons. That is, he found a way to defend his sanity, to hold his
    psyche together with an image, and to protect his ego against threatening
    invasions from the unconscious.

16. Death is the ultimate threat to the ego and its integrity. Again, Picasso
    resorted to a mask that would exorcise his fear. It is evident that he warded
    off more severe forms of psychotic disturbance by using art as therapy. In
    1932 Jung commented: "As to the future Picasso, I would rather not try my
    hand at prophecy, for this inner adventure is a hazardous affair and can

lead at any moment to a standstill or to a catastrophic bursting asunder of the conjoined opposites. Harlequin is a tragically ambiguous figure . . . *Harlequin* gives me the creeps" (Jung, "Picasso," 15:140). While Picasso's psychological life between 1932 and his death in 1972 was turbulent and subject to extreme tensions, it does not seem to have resulted in that "catastrophic bursting asunder of the conjoined opposites" that Jung feared might happen. Probably Picasso owed this to the success of his art therapy.

17. The "Liverpool dream" is reported in Jung, *Memories, Dreams, Reflections,* 197–98, at the end of the chapter entitled "Confrontation with the Unconscious." This chapter opens with Jung's break with Freud in 1912, when Jung was at a loss as to where to turn, after his massive involvement with psychoanalysis in the preceding five years came to an end. At the chapter's opening, he describes himself as dispossessed, as having no orienting myth. With this 1928 dream, he concludes the chapter by announcing that in it he at last had glimpsed the beginnings of his personal myth, the image and psychic reality of the self.

18. Stein, *Jung's Treatment of Christianity,* argues that Jung became a therapist to the Christian tradition, playing a shamanic role as healer.

19. Edward Edinger has written on this subject in many places, most completely and importantly in his *The New God Image* (Wilmette, Ill.: Chiron Publications, 1996), which is an extended commentary on several of Jung's late letters on the formation of a new God image.

20. This critique begins in Victor White's book review of Jung's *Answer to Job* ("Jung on Job," *Blackfriars* 36 [1955]: 52–60) and finds its most recent statement in Eli Weisstub, "Questions to Jung on 'Answer to Job,'" *Journal of Analytical Psychology* 38 (Oct. 1993): 397–418.

21. Jung, *Memories, Dreams, Reflections,* 223.

22. Ibid.

23. Ibid., 224.

24. Ibid.

25. Ibid., 183.

26. Ibid., 224.

27. Ibid., 225.

28. This is Jung's metaphor, from the prologue to his *Memories, Dreams, Reflections,* 4.

Epilogue

1. Hillary Rodham Clinton, *It Takes a Village: And Other Lessons Children Teach Us* (New York: Simon & Schuster, 1996), is a voice crying in the wilderness. This woman's effort to direct attention to a burning issue of our day—the care and education of young children amid the social and cultural crisis in America today—is to be applauded, even if it is unlikely to result in much improvement in the tragic situations experienced by so many youngsters, especially in urban neighborhoods and schools. The problems are deeply structural, but they are insoluble until a collective change of heart and vision occurs that will support remedial efforts on a massive scale. The "village" is a concept that finds little resonance in a time when overwhelming emphasis is placed upon the solitary ego and its immediate interests and attachments.

BIBLIOGRAPHY

Apuleius. *The Golden Ass.* Oxford, England: Oxford University Press, 1995.

Beebe, John. *Integrity in Depth.* College Station: Texas A&M University Press, 1992.

Benjamin, Jessica. *Like Subjects, Love Objects.* New Haven, Conn.: Yale University Press, 1995.

Bollas, Christopher. *The Shadow of the Object.* New York: Columbia University Press, 1987.

Bonafoux, Pascal. *Rembrandt: Master of the Portrait.* New York: Harry N. Abrams, 1990.

Carotenuto, Aldo. *Secret Symmetry: Sabina Spielrein Between Freud and Jung.* New York: Pantheon, 1982; rev. ed., 1983.

————. *Tagebuch einer heimlichen Symmetrie: Sabina Spielrein zwischen Jung und Freud.* Freiburg im Breisgau, Germany: Kore, 1986.

Chapman, H. Perry. *Rembrandt's Self-Portraits.* Princeton, N.J.: Princeton University Press, 1990.

Chevalier, Jean, and Alain Gheerbrant. *A Dictionary of Symbols.* Oxford, England: Blackwell Publisher, 1994.

Cornford, F. M. *The Unwritten Philosophy and Other Essays.* Cambridge, England: Cambridge University Press, 1950.

Edinger, Edward. *The New God Image.* Wilmette, Ill.: Chiron Publications, 1996.

Erikson, Erik. *Identity: Youth and Crisis.* New York: W. W. Norton, 1968.

————. *The Life Cycle Completed: A Review.* New York: W. W. Norton, 1982.

Fordham, Michael. *Explorations into the Self.* London: Academic Press, 1985.

Freedman, Ralph. *Life of a Poet: Rainer Maria Rilke.* New York: Farrar, Straus and Giroux, 1996.

Gill, Merton. *Psychoanalysis in Transition.* Hillsdale, N.J.: Analytic Press, 1994.

Guggenbühl-Craig, Adolf. *Marriage: Dead or Alive*. Dallas, Tex.: Spring Publications, 1975.

Hayman, Ronald. *Kafka*. New York: Oxford University Press, 1982.

Holland, W. J. *The Butterfly Book*. Garden City, N.Y.: Doubleday, 1949.

Jung, Carl Gustav. *Aion*. In *The Collected Works of C. G. Jung*, vol. 9. Princeton, N.J.: Princeton University Press, 1968.

———. *Analytical Psychology. Notes to the Seminar Held 1925*. Princeton, N.J.: Princeton University Press, 1989.

———. *Answer to Job*. In *Psychology and Religion: West and East*. In *The Collected Works of C. G. Jung*, vol. 11. Princeton, N.J.: Princeton University Press, 1969.

———. "Commentary on *The Secret of the Golden Flower*." In *Alchemical Studies*. In *The Collected Works of C. G. Jung*, vol. 13. Princeton, N.J.: Princeton University Press, 1967.

———. "Marriage as a Psychological Relationship." In *The Development of Personality*. In *The Collected Works of C. G. Jung*, vol. 17. Princeton, N.J.: Princeton University Press, 1964.

———. *Memories, Dreams, Reflections*. Recorded and edited by Aniela Jaffé. New York: Vintage Books, 1961.

———. "Picasso." In *The Spirit in Man, Art, and Literature*. In *The Collected Works of C. G. Jung*, vol. 15. Princeton, N.J.: Princeton University Press, 1966.

———. "Problems of Modern Psychotherapy." In *The Practice of Psychotherapy*. In *The Collected Works of C. G. Jung*, vol. 16. Princeton, N.J.: Princeton University Press, 1966.

———. "The Psychology of the Transference." In *The Practice of Psychotherapy*. In *The Collected Works of C. G. Jung*, vol. 16. Princeton, N.J.: Princeton University Press, 1966.

———. *Psychology of the Unconscious*. Princeton, N.J.: Princeton University Press, 1991.

———. *Symbols of Transformation*. In *The Collected Works of C. G. Jung*, vol. 5. Princeton, N.J.: Princeton University Press, 1967.

———. "Transformation Symbolism in the Mass." In *Psychology and Religion*. In *The Collected Works of C. G. Jung*, vol. 11. Princeton, N.J.: Princeton University Press, 1969.

———. *Two Essays in Analytical Psychology*. In *The Collected Works of C. G. Jung*, vol. 7. Princeton, N.J.: Princeton University Press, 1966.

————. *Wandlungen und Symbole der Libid.* Leipzig and Vienna: Franz Deuticke, 1912.

Kerr, John. *A Most Dangerous Method: The Story of Jung, Freud, and Sabina Spielrein.* New York: Knopf, 1993.

Klots, Alexander Barrett. *The World of Butterflies and Moths.* New York: McGraw-Hill, 1950.

Kohut, Heinz. *The Analysis of the Self.* New York: International Universities Press, 1971.

Lakoff, George, and Mark Johnson. *Metaphors We Live By.* Chicago: University of Chicago Press, 1980.

Leppmann, Wolfgang. *Rilke: A Life.* New York: Fromm International, 1984.

Lifton, Robert Jay. *The Protean Self.* New York: Basic Books, 1993.

McGuire, William. *The Freud-Jung Letters.* Princeton, N.J.: Princeton University Press, 1974.

Meier, C. A. *Healing Dream and Ritual: Ancient Incubation and Modern Psychotherapy.* Evanston, Ill.: Northwestern University Press, 1967.

Mitchell, Stephen, ed. *The Selected Poetry of Rainer Maria Rilke.* Translated by Stephen Mitchell. New York: Random House, 1982.

Portmann, Adolf. "Metamorphosis in Animals: The Transformations of the Individual and the Type." In *Man and Transformation,* edited by Joseph Campbell, 297–325. New York: Bollingen Foundation, 1964.

Prater, Donald. *A Ringing Glass: The Life of Rainer Maria Rilke.* Oxford, England: Clarendon Press, 1986.

Richardson, John. *A Life of Picasso.* 2 vols. New York: Random House, 1991 and 1996.

Rilke, Rainer Maria. *Duino Elegies.* Translated by David Oswald. Einsiedeln, Switzerland: Daimon Verlag, 1992.

Rosen, David H. *Transforming Depression: Healing the Soul Through Creativity.* New York: Penguin, 1996.

Shorter Oxford English Dictionary. Oxford, England: Clarendon Press, 1973.

Stein, Murray. *In MidLife.* Dallas, Tex.: Spring Publications, 1983.

————. *Jung's Treatment of Christianity.* Wilmette, Ill.: Chiron Publications, 1985.

Varnedoe, Kirk. "Picasso's Self-Portraits." In *Picasso and Portraiture: Representation and Transformation.* Edited by William Rubin, 110–79. New York: Museum of Modern Art, 1996.

von Franz, Marie-Louise. *Puer Aeternus: A Psychological Study of the Adult Struggle with the Paradise of Childhood.* 2d ed. Santa Monica, Calif.: Sigo Press, 1981.

Weisstub, Eli. "Questions to Jung on 'Answer to Job.'" *Journal of Analytical Psychology* 38 (Oct. 1993): 397–418.

White, Christopher. *Rembrandt.* London: Thames and Hudson, 1984.

INDEX

active imagination technique, 44–47, 48

adaptation, cultural/social, 9–10, 13–16, 78, 136

Adler, Alfred, 78

adolescence: clinging to, 14; environmental factors in transformation during, 72; Jung's analysis of changes in, 7–8; resistance to, 13; and sexual identity, 10, 150*n* 2

adulthood, development in, 7–10. *See also* early adulthood; midlife transformation

African symbology, 126, 128–29, 140

afterlife, skepticism about, 17

Age of Aquarius, xx, 138

aging, 10, 13–14, 141

Aion, 45, **47**

Aion (Jung), 137–38

analogical thinking, 6, 10–12, 41, 149–50*n* 2, 150*n* 4

analyst, role of, 75–76, 79, 80–83, 99. *See also* countertransference

analytical psychology: analysis of therapeutic relationship, 75–84; basis for, 55–56; and depression treatment, 150*n* 5; dream interpretation approach, 63–65; Jung's contribution to, 137; and life-stages theory, 7–8; philosophical basis for, 54–56;

vs. psychoanalysis, 42–43, 50–54, 65; on psychosis, 97–98; spiritual focus of, 73

analytic process. *See* therapeutic relationship

Angel, as transcendent guide, 34–36

anima, 49, 112, 129. *See also* soul

Answer to Job (Jung), 67, 138

anxiety, 13, 20. *See also* depression

Apollo, 31

Appelles, 115

Apuleius, 45

Aquarius, Age of, xx, 138

archetypal images: impact on youth, 49–50; mother as, 31, 33–34, 50, 67, 138–39; and Platonic Forms, 35, 50, 54, 55, 56–57; power of classical, 136; rebirth, 93–94; as shield for consciousness, 126, 128–29, 133, 157*n* 15; transformation of, 67–68, 138–39; transformative role of, xxiii, 26, 35–37, 41, 52, 85–86, 120, 145–46. *See also* transformative images

archetypal self, experience of, 97, 138. *See also* deification

art as expression of transformation: Picasso, 120–33; Rembrandt, 109–20

Auden, W. H., xii

balance, need for psychological, 54–55

Beauty (Platonic form), 50, 55

Beethoven, Ludwig van, 106

bible, 59–60, 61, 130

biology, and human transformation, 18–20, 140–42

Bollingen tower, 139–41

borderline personality disorder, 51

Burghölzli Klinik, 53–54, 75

butterfly metaphor: and transformation of self, 6, 16, 18–19, 41, 149–50*n* 2; usefulness of, 10–12, 150*n* 4

Carotenuto, Aldo, 76

centeredness, 137

change, cultural, acceleration of, xx. *See also* modernity

change, personal. *See* transformation, psychological

character, role in transformation, 108, 120–21

Château de Muzot, 28, 38

childhood, 7, 10, 15–16, 24–25, 31

Christ, Jesus, 45–46, 58–62

Christianity: formative power of, 25; Jungian critique of, 58–63; Jung's transformation of, 67–68, 138–39; as transformational, 128, 130; transubstantiation, 36–37; treatment of archetypal images, 48

circle, as symbol of eternity, 116

City of Pain, 34

collective consciousness, integration of, xxii–xxiii

collective images. *See* archetypal images

collective imagination, 97

collective influences, scope of, xxi, 143–48. *See also* culture

collective unconscious: in relationships, 101, 104–105; as source of transformative images, 56, 71; tap-

ping into, 46–47, 104, 131; transformation of, 144–48

collective uniformity, and demise of individual, xxii, 146, 148

"Commentary on *The Secret of the Golden Flower*" (Jung), 137

communities, transformative relationships within, 104

concept-building, metaphors and, 11

concrete thinking, developmental progress from, 35–37, 55

confession stage of therapy, 77

consciousness: archetypal images as shields for, 126, 128–29, 133, 157*n* 15; bringing anima to, 49; and differentiation, 65; integration of collective, xxii–xxiii; multiple centers of, 109, 125; in relationship dynamic, 70, 80–82; transformation to new, 22

context of transformational process, 72–73, 111. *See also* relationship, transformative

Cornford, F. M., 45, 56, 57

countertransference, 73–75, 82–83, 154–55*n* 20. *See also* transference

couple relationship, as shaper of adult imago, 104–105. *See also* relationship, transformative

creativity: and midlife transformation, 25, 26, 34, 106–109, 123; as shield against unconscious, 126, 128–29, 133, 157*n* 15; and tapping of collective unconscious, 131

culture: adaptation to, 9–10, 13–16, 78, 136; as archetypally based, 52; deconstruction of, 144–45; development within, 8; and ego, 159*n* 1; and limits on identity, 108, 109; and midlife transformation, 27; and psychological health, 56–63; scope of influence, xxi, 143–48;

transcendence of, 116, 119–20, 123, 128–29, 135; transformation of, xx, xxi–xxiii, 67, 147–48. *See also* modernity
Cusa, Nicholas, 97

death: fear of, 131–33, **132;** transformational emotions concerning, 29–34; as ultimate transformation, 10, 16
deconstruction of culture, 144–45
deification: Jung's, 45–46, 136–38; of Mary, Mother of Jesus, 67, 138–39; Picasso's, 130–31; Rembrandt's, 116, 118; through transformation, 57, 71; traditional religious view of, 9; in unconscious couple, 93–94, 97; universal availability of, 146
Demeter, 57
democratization of transformation, 146
depression, 13, 20, 87–91, 150n 5
depth psychology. *See* analytical psychology; psychoanalysis
desire, as source of human energy, 34
destiny, individual, 65–66, 107–109
developmental issues: concrete to symbolic thinking, 35–37, 55; and cultural influences, xxi; imago creation, 14–15, 71–72; stages of life, 7–8; timing of transformative phases, 10; variations in individual potential, 143–44, 146–48, 156n 2. *See also* adolescence; childhood; early adulthood; midlife transformation
Diotima, 55
dirges, origin of, 31
disidentification from archetypal images, 48
disintegration, psychological, 51, 66–67. *See also* psychopathology

dream images, as transformative, 5–6, 41, 63–65, 150–51n 9
drives, instinctual. *See* instinctual drives
duality. *See* opposites, union of
Duino Castle, 25–26
Duino Elegies (Rilke), 25–26, 28–38
Dulles, Allan, 40

early adulthood: achievement focus, 110–12; ego development in, 13; grandiosity in, 111, 117, 125; idealism in, 114; as latency period, 71; and multiplicity of styles, 124; tasks of, 135–36; transformative image's impact in, 49–50
education stage of therapy, 78
ego: artistic representation of, 141; cultural overemphasis on, 159n 1; death as threat to, 157–58n 16; in early adulthood, 13; mastery of, 73–74, 78; in Picasso's work, 124–25; in therapeutic relationship, 80–82; transcendence of, 71, 114; and unconscious, 79, 83–84, 97–98
elegy, poetic use of, 29
Eleusinian mysteries, 56–57
elucidation stage of therapy, 77–78
embodiment, of self, 140–42
entertainment, vs. transformation, 148
environmental factors in transformation, 72–73, 111. *See also* culture; relationship, transformative
epigenetic progression, 8
Erikson, Erik, 8, 10
Eros, 55, 72
eternity, and psychological transcendence of time, 98, 102, 116, 120, 138

faith in transformative relationship, 92

interactive matrix in analysis, 76, 79, 153*n* 6
internalization of analyst, 99
interpretation, 73, 75–78
intimacy, difficulties in expressing, 70
intimate relationship. *See* relationship, transformative
irrational union, 84, 86

Jesus of Nazareth, 45–46, 58–62. *See also* Christianity
Johnson, Mark, 11
Jung, Carl Gustav: break with Freud, 42–43, 50–54, 65, 154*n* 10; childhood of, 24–25; on deconstruction of Western culture, 145; dream interpretation approach, 63–65; gnosticism of, 155*n* 1; and lifestages, 7–8; and marriage as transformative, 100, 102–103; midlife transformation of, 23, 42–46, 48–49, 134–42; philosophical basis of theory, 43, 54–56; on psychosis, 97–98; religion as transformative experience, 57–63; and Spielrein case, 75–76; transformation in therapeutic relationship, 74, 76–84; transformation of religious images, 67–68, 138–39; on wholeness in relationships, 69
Jung, Emma, 102–103
Jung, Paul, 102
The Jung Cult (Noll), 43

Kafka, Franz, xix
Khokhlova, Olga, 129, 131
kinship libido, 84, 101–102

Lakoff, George, 11
lamentation, 29–34
latent psychological structures, 14 15, 71

Leontocephalus, 46
Les Demoiselles d'Avignon (Picasso), 128
libido, 51, 84, 101–102. *See also* instinctual drives
Lifton, Robert Jay, 8
liminality, xx, 7, 20, 27–28
Linus, 31
love as universal link, 64–65

marriage, 100–104
Mary, Mother of Jesus, 67, 138–39
masks, as shields for consciousness, 126, 128–29, 133
materialism, developmental uses of, 111–12, 121
Mellon, William Larimar, Jr., 39–40, 46
Memories, Dreams and Reflections (Jung), 48, 102
Mennonites, 118
metamorphosis. *See* transformation, psychological
metaphor: explanatory function of, 10–12, 150*n* 4; transformative image as, 6, 16, 18–19, 41, 149–50*n* 2
Metaphors We Live By (Lakoff and Johnson), 11
midlife transformation: catalytic images for, 39–49, 40–41; and creativity, 25, 26, 34; cultural influence on, 27; definition of, 19–20; and depression, 13, 20; and identity development, 8; Jung's, 23, 42–46, 48–49, 134–42; resistance to, 13–15; Rilke's 23–38; and self-realization, 37, 107–108; and spiritual growth, 22–23; timing of, 9–10, 18–19, 79; traumatic beginnings of, 111; and true self, 10, 15–16, 71
Minotaur, 130–31
Mithraic mythology, 45–46, **47,** 137–38

modernity: Picasso as embodiment of, 145; and spiritual fragmentation, 46, 62, 121–22, 125, 128, 133, 134; transformations of, xx, xxi–xxii

mother: as archetype, 31, 33–34, 50, 57, 67, 138–39; as formative influence, 24–25

motivation, sources of human, 51–52. *See also* instinctual drives

mourning, as transformational theme, 29–34

music, 31

mutual soul, development of, 86–87

mutual transference, 83, 84. *See also* countertransference; transference

Muzot, Château de, 28, 38

Mysterium Coniunctionis, 137

mythology: African, 126, 128–29, 140; and children's dream imagery, 150–51*n* 9; Greek, 31, 56–57, 115, 128–31; need for new, 67–68, 158*n* 17; Persian, 45–46, 47, 137–38; and soul as butterfly, 16–17; transformative role of, 52–54, 115. *See also* deification; religious experience; spirituality

neurosis, 42–43, 74. *See also* depression

nihilism, rise of, 145

Noll, Richard, 43–44, 45

noumenal essence in art, 127–28, 129

obituaries, as sources of transformative moments, 41–42

object relations, vs. archetypal theory, 154*n* 18

object-to-symbol transformation, 35–37, 55

Office of Strategic Services (OSS), 39–40

old age, 10, 141

opposites, union of: in Christianity, 139; individual vs. collective image, xxii, 112, 147; Jung's architectural expression of, 140; Picasso's artistic expression of, 125, 129, 131; of time and eternity, 98, 102, 116, 120, 138; in unconscious couple, 95–97, **96**

Orpheus, 31

OSS (Office of Strategic Services), 39–40

pathology, and difficulties of transformation, 51, 66–67, 74, 156*n* 2

Paul of Tarsus, 59–60, 118

Persian mythology, 45–46, **47,** 137–38

Peter Pan Syndrome, 13, 150*n* 6

Philemon, 140

Picasso, Pablo, 120–33, **127, 130, 132,** 145, 157–58*n* 13–16

Plato, 50, 54–57

Platonic Forms, 35, 50, 54, 55, 56–57

pleasure principle, 54–55. *See also* sexuality

poetry, 26, 27–28, 34, 38

polarity of opposites. *See* opposites, union of

Portmann, Adolf, 18, 19

postmodernism, 141, 144

power principle, 54, 55, 79, 111

Preiswerk, Helene, 102

"Problems of Modern Psychotherapy" (Jung), 76–79

prophecy vs. fantasy, 45

Protean self, 8

Prozac, 13

psyche, nature of, 53–54, 70

psychic energy: nature of, 34, 51, 53; and religious experience, 52, 57–58; and transformation, 107–109, 122–

23, 133–34; and transformative image, 50, 56

psychoanalysis: analyst's role, 75–76; pleasure principle focus of, 54–55; sexuality focus of, 42–43, 50–51, 53, 72–73; and stages of life, 7; transference theory, 73–74, 77–78

Psychological Types (Jung), 136

psychology. *See* analytical psychology; developmental issues; psychoanalysis

"The Psychology of the Transference" (Jung), 80

Psychology of the Unconscious (Jung), 42, 43, 51, 136

psychopathology, and difficulties of transformation, 51, 66–67, 74, 97–98, 156n 2

psychosis, Jung's definition of, 97–98

psychotherapy. *See* therapeutic relationship

pupation, as central to transformation, 17–18

Quaternity vs. Trinity, 138

rebirth archetype, 93–94

Rebis symbol, 93–97, **96**, 101–102, 103–104, 129

reflective approach to archetypal images, 48

Reformation, 60–61

regression, cultural, 144

Reinhart, Werner, 28

relationship, transformative: collective, 104–105; Jung's insight into, 75–84; mutually unconscious, 80, 84–98, **87–96**; personal, 99–104; transference theory, 73–75; wholeness as goal of, 69–70

religious experience: active imagination as, 46–47; modern loss of, 62,

128, 133, 134; personal nature of, 155n 1; and Rembrandt's art, 114; transcendence of traditional, 128; transformation of, 67–68, 138–39, 144; as transformative, 41, 45–46, 52, 57–63, 65. *See also* Christianity; spirituality

Rembrandt van Rijn, 109–20, **113, 115, 117, 119,** 121

Renaissance, 60–61

repression, 153n 1

Republic (Plato), 54

Richardson, John, 122, 126

Rijn, Harmon Gerriszoon van, 109

Rijn, Rembrandt van. *See* Rembrandt van Rijn

Rijn, Titus van, 116

Rilke, Rainer Maria, 23–28

Rosarium Philosophorum, 80, 84–97, **87–96**

Saint Paul, 59–60, 118

sanity, artistic expression as defense of, 126, 128–29, 133, 157n 15

schizophrenia, as biological disorder, 74

Schweitzer, Albert, 40–41, 46, 50

second half of life: processes of, 8; and self-realization, 37, 107–108; as transformation focus in therapy, 79; transition to, 18–19; and wisdom imago, 103. *See also* midlife transformation

self: as archetypal factor, 97, 138; discovery of true, 8–9, 10, 15–16, 71; vs. ego, 9, 97–98; embodiment of, 140–42; as Jung's focus, 137–38. *See also* imago, self; self-realization; unconscious

self-portrait, as illumination of imago, 110, 124

conscious as source of, 56, 71; cultural application of, 57–63, 67–68; divine design in, 106–107; as metaphors, 6, 16, 18–19, 41, 149–50n 2; and midlife psyche, 39–49; as motivational source, 50–54; and personal wholeness, 54–56, 63–66; in relationship, 97; and young psyche, 49–50. *See also* archetypal images

transubstantiation, 36–37

Trinity, 59–60, 67–68, 138

unconscious: active imagination as gateway to, 44–45; chaos of, 137, 145; collective, 46–47, 56, 71, 101, 104–105, 131, 144–48; consciousness as protection from, 91; creativity as shield against, 126, 128–29, 133, 157n 15; and ego, 83–84, 97–98; as imago source, 71; Picasso's revelation of, 127–28; as psychic energy source, 53; psychological journey to, 33–34; relational couple as, 80, 84–102, **87–96**; unitary nature of, 64–65, 86–87

union: archetypal, 94–97, **96,** 99; of body and spirit, 140–42; in unconscious relationship, 84, 86–87, 103. *See also* opposites, union of; wholeness

unitary nature of unconscious, 64–65, 86–87

Uylenburgh, Saskia, 111

Varnedoe, Kirk, 124

Virgin Mother, 67, 138–39

vocational mission, sense of, 25

Walter, Marie-Thérèse, 129, 131

Wandlungen und Symbole der Libido (Jung), 42, 43, 51, 136

Western culture: and deification idea, 9; Holocaust's impact on, 66–67; and modernity, 120, 122–23, 134; transformation of, 60–61, 144–48

White, Victor, 139

wholeness: and dream imagery, 63; Jung's achievement of, 141; as moral guide to worth of religion, 58–59; need for collective, 147–48; Picasso's expression of, 131; as psychological goal, 55, 56; in relationships, 69–70, 95, 97, 101, 103; in transformative process, 54–56, 63–66, 71, 85, 108–109. *See also* integration, psychological

will, as source of psychic energy, 34

Winterthur, 28

wisdom principle, 54, 55, 103

world culture, transformation of, xx, xxi–xxiii, 67, 147–48

Wunderly-Volkart, Nanny, 28

wu wei, 92

youthful dead, 30–31

Zeitgeist, 123

Zeuxis, 116–17

Zrwanakarana, 45

Zurich, Lake, 139

Carolyn and Ernest Fay Series in Analytical Psychology
David H. Rosen, General Editor
Texas A&M University Press

Beebe, John. *Integrity in Depth*, 1992.
Kast, Verena. *Joy, Inspiration, and Hope*, 1991.
Kawai, Hayao. *Buddhism and the Art of Psychotherapy*, 1996.
Stevens, Anthony. *The Two-Million-Year-Old Self*, 1993.
Woodman, Marion. *The Stillness Shall Be the Dancing: Feminine and Masculine in Emerging Balance* (audio), 1994.
Young-Eisendrath, Polly. *Gender and Desire: Uncursing Pandora*, 1997.